L. C Skey, à Kempis Thomas

Christe Eleison

A short office of meditation and prayerfor every day iv lent

L. C Skey, à Kempis Thomas

Christe Eleison
A short office of meditation and prayerfor every day iv lent

ISBN/EAN: 9783741194351

Manufactured in Europe, USA, Canada, Australia, Japa

Cover: Foto ©Lupo / pixelio.de

Manufactured and distributed by brebook publishing software (www.brebook.com)

L. C Skey, à Kempis Thomas

Christe Eleison

CHRISTE ELEISON.

"Christe Eleison."

A SHORT OFFICE OF
MEDITATION AND PRAYER FOR EVERY DAY IN LENT.

WITH SELECTIONS FROM THE "IMITATION OF CHRIST,"
BY THOMAS A KEMPIS.

Part I.—"Dying Unto Sin."
Part II.—"Living Unto Christ."

"As dying, and behold we live."
2 COR. VI. 9.

BY

L. C. SKEY,

AUTHOR OF "COMFORTED OF GOD," "THE PERFECT DAY," ETC.

Dedicated by permission to
H. P. LIDDON, D.D.

London:
SKEFFINGTON & SON, 163, PICCADILLY.
1887.

TO THE REV.

HENRY PARRY LIDDON, D.D.,

CANON OF S. PAUL'S CATHEDRAL,

I HAVE BEEN PERMITTED TO INSCRIBE THIS BOOK

IN TOKEN OF MY REVERENCE FOR HIM

AND FOR THE

WORK HE IS DOING IN THE CHURCH OF GOD.

Introductory Chapter.

My desire in compiling this book is to try to give some help to those who wish to spend their Lent with Jesus.

The forty days fast, if we pass it as much as possible in the seclusion of the desert, alone with Jesus, must indeed be a time of strengthening to our souls, fortifying them to encounter their great spiritual foe, and preparing them to join at Easter in the Lamb's High Festival. We may be very sure that if, with the dear Master, we deny ourselves, and fast and pray, to us, too, an angel will come to feed us with the Bread of Heaven, and to give us to drink of the Chalice of Salvation.

"Christe Eleison," shall be our antiphon this Lent. The cry for mercy shall be ever on our lips and in our hearts. Then I hope we may find in this book some words each day which may give new force to the daily prayer, and may touch the innermost needs of every heart.

The chapters are intended to be used as a short office to be said at any time during the day, but perhaps especially in the morning hours, because it is hoped that at least the words of Jesus, which form a part of it, may remain in the minds of those who read them through the day.

It is also hoped that possibly the book may be found useful for services in mission or school rooms. It will, I hope, endear to us all the marvellous beauty of the words of the "Imitation of Christ."

Should this book succeed in making anyone love and study the "Imitation" more than they have hitherto done, it will not have been written in vain.

The suffrages and the "Lord's Prayer," placed at the commencement of the first chapter, are intended to be said before each day's meditation, but it was not thought advisable to print so many repetitions of the words.

The Litanies will be found in the People's Hymnal, except the Litany of Patience, which has been translated expressly for this book from the French, and will be found in the Appendix.

It is earnestly desired that the short Psalm and Lesson for each day should be read after the meditation, as the office will be incomplete without them.

I make my apology for undertaking so great a task in the words of a Saint, who lived in the sixteenth century:—"In the same manner as it would delight a king to see a shepherd on whom he had bestowed some favour, expressing astonishment on viewing his embroidered robe, and pondering how it was made, and what it was, so we women are not to be so hindered from enjoying the riches of our Lord, and from speaking of them, as to conceal them entirely, thinking that thereby we do well. We should rather first show our writings to learned men ; and if they approve them, then communicate them to others."

May the mercy of Christ our Lord rest on all those who draw near to Him in the sacred hours of His Fasting and Temptation, His Agony and Sweat of Blood, His Cross and Passion, and His most precious Death and Burial, and may His children so mourn with Him now, that they may enjoy the Benediction of His Glorious Presence at the Feast of His Resurrection.

Of your charity, pray for the Blessing of God on my work.

NOTE.—By a mistake, which it was too late to correct, Thomas à Kempis has been spoken of as "S. Thomas," though he has not been canonized.

INDEX.

PART I.

Dying Unto Sin.

			PAGE
CHAPTER	I.	*Ash Wednesday*—Humiliation	2
,,	II.	*First Thursday in Lent*—Compunction	4
,,	III.	*First Friday in Lent*—Suffering for Sin	6
,,	IV.	*First Saturday in Lent*—Purity of Intention	8
,,	V.	*First Sunday in Lent*—Fervour	11
,,	VI.	*First Monday in Lent*—Want of Comfort in Religion	13
,,	VII.	*First Tuesday in Lent*—Patience towards ourselves	15
,,	VIII.	*Second Wednesday in Lent*—Patience towards our Brethren	17
,,	IX.	*Second Thursday in Lent*—Patience towards God	19
,,	X.	*Second Friday in Lent*—Suffering in Body	21
,,	XI.	*Second Saturday in Lent*—Quietness of Mind	23
,,	XII.	*Second Sunday in Lent*—Interior Consolations	26
,,	XIII.	*Second Monday in Lent*—Difficulties in the Way	28
,,	XIV.	*Second Tuesday in Lent*—Faults of the Saints	30
,,	XV.	*Third Wednesday in Lent*—Warfare	33
,,	XVI.	*Third Thursday in Lent*—Foes Within	35
,,	XVII.	*Third Friday in Lent*—Suffering in Mind	37
,,	XVIII.	*Third Saturday in Lent*—Obedience	39
,,	XIX.	*Third Sunday in Lent*—Light	41
,,	XX.	*Third Monday in Lent*—What holds us back?	43
,,	XXI.	*Third Tuesday in Lent*—Self-will	45
,,	XXII.	*Fourth Wednesday in Lent*—Self-love	47

		PAGE
CHAPTER XXIII.	*Fourth Thursday in Lent*—Self-indulgence	49
,, XXIV.	*Fourth Friday in Lent*—Faithfulness of God	51
,, XXV.	*Fourth Saturday in Lent*—Fear	53

PART II.

Living Unto Christ.

CHAPTER XXVI.	*Fourth Sunday in Lent*—Refreshment	58
,, XXVII.	*Fourth Monday in Lent*—Simplicity	60
,, XXVIII.	*Fourth Tuesday in Lent*—Receptivity	62
,, XXIX.	*Fifth Wednesday in Lent*—Discipleship	65
,, XXX.	*Fifth Thursday in Lent*—Friendship with Jesus	68
,, XXXI.	*Fifth Friday in Lent*—Fellowship in Suffering	71
,, XXXII.	*Fifth Saturday in Lent*—Readiness	73
,, XXXIII.	*Fifth Sunday in Lent*—The Law of Sacrifice	76
,, XXXIV.	*Fifth Monday in Lent*—Sacrifice of Love	78
,, XXXV.	*Fifth Tuesday in Lent*—Sacrifice of Thanksgiving	81
,, XXXVI.	*Sixth Wednesday in Lent*—Sacrifice of Obedience	83
,, XXXVII.	*Sixth Thursday in Lent*—Sacrifice of Praise	85
,, XXXVIII.	*Sixth Friday in Lent*—Joy of Sacrifice	88
,, XXXIX.	*Sixth Saturday in Lent*—Crown of Sacrifice	90
,, XL.	*Sunday next before Easter*—Rejoicing in the Lord	92
,, XLI.	*Monday before Easter*—The Man of Sorrows	95
,, XLII.	*Tuesday before Easter*—Betrayed	97
,, XLIII.	*Wednesday before Easter*—Despised	100
,, XLIV.	*Thursday before Easter*—Carrying His Cross	103
,, XLV.	*Good Friday*—Glorious in His Apparel	105
,, XLVI.	*Easter Eve*—Resting from His Labours	107

PART I.

Dying Unto Sin.

Lord, have mercy.
Christ, have mercy.
Lord, have mercy.

OUR FATHER, WHICH ART IN HEAVEN, HALLOWED BE THY NAME. THY KINGDOM COME. THY WILL BE DONE IN EARTH, AS IT IS IN HEAVEN. GIVE US THIS DAY OUR DAILY BREAD. AND FORGIVE US OUR TRESPASSES, AS WE FORGIVE THEM THAT TRESPASS AGAINST US. AND LEAD US NOT INTO TEMPTATION; BUT DELIVER US FROM EVIL: FOR THINE IS THE KINGDOM, THE POWER, AND THE GLORY, FOR EVER AND EVER. AMEN.

It is suggested that the above prayers be used before the meditation for each day.

Ash Wednesday.

HUMILIATION.

"I AM BROUGHT INTO SO GREAT TROUBLE AND MISERY, THAT I GO MOURNING ALL THE DAY LONG."—PSALM XXXVIII. 6.

"DUST THOU ART, AND UNTO DUST SHALT THOU RETURN."—GEN. III. 19.

"In silence and in quiet the devout soul goes forward and learns the secret of the Scriptures. There she finds floods of tears with which she may wash and cleanse herself every night, that she may become so much the more familiar with her Maker, by how much the farther she lives from all worldly tumult."   S. THOMAS A KEMPIS.

WE will begin our Lent by trying to humble ourselves before our God, in calling to mind the many and grievous sins which we have committed against Him.

We must fall down before Him as those who are dead and lie in the grave, for the stillness and silence of the grave is the last and deepest humiliation that human nature can know, as it is also the profoundest act of homage to the majesty of God.

We must remember our sins this day, and repent in dust and ashes, that so being dead unto sin, we may rise to newness of life in Christ Jesus our Lord.

Those who die have ceased to care for the pleasures and allurements of this world. They have passed away, and left all earthly treasures behind them. So should it be with us, who are dying to sin. We are passing away from it, so that we shall no longer hear its music, or see its alluring brightness. All must be left behind, in the city from which we are departing.

The grave is very silent and very still, so should our penitential acts be done in quietness and stillness before God. It is not by a "tumult" of religious efforts we can best please God, and learn His Will. The secret of the Lord is with them who possess their souls in patience, and who bow down themselves in His Presence, and keep silence before Him, that they may listen to His Voice when He speaks to their souls. Deep waters are still, it is the shallow stream which babbles as it flows.

Those who lie in the grave are unseen by men, and are "out of remembrance," so will we be content, during our Lenten fast, to be alone, and to hide ourselves in the wilderness, that in the deep seclusion of the desert we may find our Blessed Lord, and ask Him to teach us how we may encounter, and defeat, the great enemy of our souls.

Those who are in the grave are in a state of expectation, they are waiting for the coming of the Lord. So from the deep abyss of sorrow and contrition in which we lie, we must keep our longing eyes fixed on the Eastern sky, in patient expectation till the dawn of Easter shall break, and the Day Star shall arise and make our darkness to be light.

So shall the evening shadows of the first day of Lent close on us, and leave us in the silence and stillness of our deep humiliation before God.

> "Jesus, Lord of dead and living,
> Let Thy mercy rest on me,
> Grant me, too, when life is finished,
> Rest in Paradise with Thee."

Aspiration.

"Have mercy upon me, Thou Son of David."

Voice of Jesus.

"COME UNTO ME ALL YE THAT LABOUR AND ARE HEAVY LADEN."

Read *Psalm xxx.* Lesson, *Book of Jonah ii.*

Litany of Penitence.

First Thursday in Lent.

COMPUNCTION.

"I ACKNOWLEDGE MY FAULTS, AND MY SIN IS EVER BEFORE ME."—PSALM LI. 3.

"JESUS SAID, ONE OF YOU WHICH EATETH WITH ME SHALL BETRAY ME. AND THEY BEGAN TO BE VERY SORROWFUL, AND TO SAY TO HIM ONE BY ONE, IS IT I? AND ANOTHER SAID, IS IT I?"—S. MARK XIV. 18, 19.

"This is the highest and most profitable lesson, truly to know and to despise ourselves. To have no opinion of ourselves, and to think well and commendably of others, is great wisdom and high perfection.

"If thou shouldst see another openly sin, or commit some heinous crime, yet thou oughtst not to esteem thyself better: because thou knowest not how long thou mayest remain in a good state. We are all frail; but see thou think no one more frail than thyself. S. THOMAS A KEMPIS.

IF our Lenten meditations are to be blessed to us, we must take them home to our hearts, and apply them individually to our own souls.

First Thursday in Lent.

A general lament over our sinfulness, and over the wickedness of the world, will not help us so to die to sin, that we may rise to newness of life.

We must apply ourselves to search out, each his own peculiar sins, and occasions of falling, and mark them before God, even as we believe them to be recorded in His Book of Remembrance, against us.

When the voice of Jesus says so mournfully, "One of you shall betray Me," let every Christian soul ask Him, "Lord, is it I?"

We must not imagine that it is impossible for us to commit so great a sin. Alas! we do not know to what depths of iniquity we may fall, unless the grace of God sustain us. We have loved self and money too well; we have been grasping and covetous, and failed in our duty to the poor; were the temptation but a little stronger, might we not be led to betray our Lord and Master, and to put Him to an open shame?

Let this be our attitude before our Crucified Lord this day; let it be to us a day of remembrance, a day on which we accuse ourselves, and excuse our neighbours, a day on which our hearts are ever asking, in fear and trembling, "Dear Lord, is it I?"

So may we never hear the terrible sentence pronounced upon us by the voice of Judgment, "Thou art the man."

> "I saw One hanging on a Tree,
> In agonies and blood,
> Who fixed His languid eyes on me,
> As near His Cross I stood.

> "My conscience felt and owned my guilt,
> And plunged me in despair,
> I saw my sins His Blood had spilt,
> And helped to nail Him there."

Aspiration.
"*God be merciful to me a sinner.*"

Voice of Jesus.
"HIM THAT COMETH UNTO ME I WILL IN NO WISE CAST OUT."

Read *Psalm li.*   Lesson, *2 Sam. xii.*

Litany of Penitence.

First Friday in Lent.

SUFFERING FOR SIN.

"THY HAND IS HEAVY UPON ME DAY AND NIGHT."—PSALM XXXII. 4.

"THERE IS NO HEALTH IN MY FLESH BECAUSE OF THY DISPLEASURE, NEITHER IS THERE ANY REST IN MY BONES BY REASON OF MY SIN."—PSALM XXXVIII. 3.

"AND JESUS SAID UNTO THEM, SUPPOSE YE THAT THESE GALILEANS WERE SINNERS ABOVE ALL THE GALILEANS, BECAUSE THEY SUFFERED SUCH THINGS? I TELL YOU NAY."

"Son, see thou dispute not of high matters, nor of the hidden judgments of God; why this man is left thus, and this other is raised to so great a grace, or why this person is so much afflicted, and that other is so highly exalted.

"These things are above the reach of man, neither can any reason or discourse be able to penetrate into the judgments of God. When, therefore, the enemy suggests to thee such things as these, or thou hearest curious men enquiring into them, let thy answer be, 'Thou art just, O Lord, and Thy judgment is right.'

"Thy judgments are to be feared, not to be searched into, for they are incomprehensible to human misunderstanding."   *S. THOMAS A KEMPIS.*

First Friday in Lent.

ALL the Fridays in the year are, in the mind of the Church, hallowed by the shadow of the Cross, therefore, on the Fridays in Lent, we will meditate on the deep mystery of suffering.

We must be careful, in the first place, not to consider the word suffering as synonymous with punishment. When we are punished, of course we suffer, but suffering is by no means to be considered always as punishment. It is rather the loving and reassuring touch of the Hand of God laid upon us, to convince us of our sonship to Him, and of our union with our Blessed Lord in His Adorable Passion.

This it is to "suffer according to the will of God," but there is another kind of suffering, which is more bitter, the pain caused us by our sins. This is of two kinds—the suffering which the sins themselves bring on us, and the penitential pain which the remembrance of our sins causes us, when the grace of God has called us to repentance.

But all suffering of whatever kind, is intended to purify, and raise us higher, in our Christian life. Even the pain brought on us by sin, has a good work to do in us ; a work of humiliation, cleansing, and making us patient. Therefore, we see that even the lowest form of suffering bears with it the Benediction of God to the faithful soul, even as the curse on Eve's transgression carried to a sin-struck world, the highest of all blessings, in the glorious promise of the Incarnation of the Son of God.

And now let us take to ourselves a warning, never to judge our neighbour because we see that he suffers. We cannot tell in what manner the Hand of God is resting on him, therefore let us give him our pity and our prayers, and then turn our thoughts to ourselves, and pray that the judgment of God may lead us to repentance.

> "O, is it not wonderful, servant of God,
> That He should have honoured us so with His love,
> That the sorrows of life should but shorten the road
> That leads to Himself, and the mansions above?
>
> That God hath once whispered a word in thine ear,
> Or sent thee from Heaven one sorrow for sin,
> Is enough for a life, to banish all fear,
> And to turn into peace all the troubles within."

Aspiration.
"*Lord, save me.*"

Voice of Jesus.
"WHOSOEVER WILL COME AFTER ME, LET HIM DENY HIMSELF, AND TAKE UP HIS CROSS AND FOLLOW ME."

Read *Psalm xxii.* Lesson, *Job xxiii.*

Litany of the Passion.

First Saturday in Lent.

PURITY OF INTENTION.

"AN OFFERING OF A FREE HEART WILL I GIVE THEE, AND PRAISE THY NAME O LORD, BECAUSE IT IS SO COMFORTABLE."—PSALM LIV. 6.

" IF ANY MAN COME TO ME, AND HATE NOT HIS FATHER, AND MOTHER, AND WIFE, AND CHILDREN, AND BRETHREN, AND SISTERS, YEA, AND HIS OWN LIFE ALSO, HE CANNOT BE MY DISCIPLE."—S. LUKE XV. 26.

"*With two wings a man is lifted up above earthly things, that is simplicity and purity. Simplicity must be in the intention; purity in the* affection. *No good action will hinder thee if thou be free from individual affections.*

"*If thou intendest and seekest nothing else but the will of God, and the profit of thy neighbour, thou shalt enjoy internal liberty.*

"*If thy heart were right, then every creature would be to thee a looking-glass of life, and a book of holy doctrine.*

"*There is no creature so little and contemptible, as not to manifest the goodness of God.*" S. THOMAS A KEMPIS.

GOD has given man a free will, in order that he may have the blessedness of making his choice of God. We are not forced to serve Him; indeed, He will accept no compulsory service, at our hands.

Convinced of our own unworthiness and helplessness, and of His love towards us, as manifested in the Life and Death of our Blessed Lord, and penetrated with deep thankfulness to Him, we must offer Him the best gift we have to bestow, the offering of a free heart, full of love and praise.

A free heart is a heart unbound from the trammels of society and conventionality. Not that we should study to be remarked for singularity, far from it, but that we should refuse to obey those social laws which are opposed to the simple rules of life, laid down for us by our Divine Master.

A free heart is a simple heart. It believes the Truth of God "as a little child," and serves Him with an unquestioning obedience. It does not exercise itself in matters which are too high for it, and is untroubled by doubts about the Faith.

A free heart is a pure heart. It is free from all inordinate affections for the things of earth, and can therefore rise to greater heights of love for Him Whom now we see not, but in Whom we can rejoice with joy unspeakable. The utterance of the pure heart is this—"Whom have I in Heaven but Thee, and what is there upon earth that I desire in comparison of Thee ?"

We do not realize what a tremendous thing it is to choose Christ. Our Loving Master would not make our way more hard than necessary, yet His words are almost terrible in their solemn call to renounce *all* that is dear to self.

Let us this day consider her, to whom old custom dedicated the Saturday in every week, the Virgin Mother of God. Like her, may we answer the Divine call out of a pure heart and love unfeigned, "Behold the handmaid of the Lord, be it unto me according to Thy word."

> "O, for a heart to praise my God,
>   A heart from sin set free ;
> A heart that's sprinkled with the blood
>   So freely shed for me.
>
> A heart resigned, submissive, meek,
>   My dear Redeemer's throne,
> Where only Christ is heard to speak,
>   Where Jesus reigns alone."

Aspiration.
"*I will follow Thee whithersoever Thou goest.*"

Voice of Jesus.
"BLESSED ARE THE PURE IN HEART, FOR THEY SHALL SEE GOD."

Read the *Magnificat*. Lesson, *1 Samuel ii. 1 to 12*.

Litany of the Holy Ghost.

First Sunday in Lent.

FERVOUR.

"AS FOR ME, I WILL CALL UPON GOD, AND THE LORD SHALL SAVE ME."—PSALM LV. 17.

"BEHOLD, NOW IS THE ACCEPTED TIME : BEHOLD, NOW IS THE DAY OF SALVATION."—2 COR. VI. 2.

"*Always remember thine end, and that time once lost never returns.*

"*If thou beginnest to grow lukewarm, thou wilt begin to be uneasy.*

"*But if thou givest thyself to fervour, thou shalt find great peace : and the grace of God, and love of virtue, will make thee feel less labour.*

"*He that does not shun small defects by little and little, falls into greater.*

"*Thou wilt always rejoice in the evening, if thou spend the day profitably.*

"*Watch over thyself, stir up thyself, admonish thyself.*

"*The greater violence thou offerest to thyself, the greater progress thou wilt make.*"   *S. THOMAS A KEMPIS.*

PEOPLE are greatly mistaken who imagine that salvation is a thing only of the future, which will not affect us until after our death.

Surely if we do not reach a state of salvation while we live, we shall not attain to it when we die.

Our Blessed Lord lived on earth for more than thirty years, that He might set before us the pattern of a Perfect Life, and yet men talk and live, as if the Death of Jesus was the only gift He gave His children. If in our death we hope to share the blessings which His Passion has purchased for us, we must follow Him day by day through life.

From the time that He calls us, we must leave His side never more.

True, the loving Master's Arms are stretched wide to receive all who come to Him. The sinner who comes at his last moment, shall find admission there, if, even then at the eleventh hour, he heeds the call of God, but how can we expect the like mercy, who have neglected it from our youth up? Those last moments, to which we are looking to make our peace with God, may never come.

The present moment, the all-important *now*, is all we can call our own.

Let us give it to God, and He will save us.

> "Why, O Blessed Jesus Christ
> Should I not love Thee well,
> Not for the sake of winning Heaven,
> Or of escaping hell?
>
> Not with the hope of gaining aught,
> Not seeking a reward,
> But as Thyself hast loved me,
> O, ever-loving Lord;
>
> Even so I love Thee, and will love,
> And in Thy praise will sing,
> Because Thou art my Lord and God,
> And my eternal King."

Aspiration.
"*Lord tell us when shall these things be?*"

Voice of Jesus.
"WATCH, THEREFORE; FOR YE KNOW NEITHER THE DAY NOR THE HOUR WHEREIN THE SON OF MAN COMETH."

Read *Psalm cxxxii.* Lesson, *Hab. ii.*, *to v. 14.*

Litany of our Lord Jesus Christ.

First Monday in Lent.

WANT OF COMFORT IN RELIGION.

"MINE EYES LONG SORE FOR THY WORD: SAYING, O WHEN WILT THOU COMFORT ME."—PSALM CXIX. 82.

"I SAY THE TRUTH IN CHRIST, I LIE NOT, MY CONSCIENCE ALSO BEARING ME WITNESS IN THE HOLY GHOST."

"THAT I HAVE GREAT HEAVINESS AND CONTINUAL SORROW IN MY HEART."

"FOR I COULD WISH THAT MYSELF WERE ACCURSED FROM CHRIST FOR MY BRETHREN."—ROMANS IX. 1, 2, 3.

"It is much, very much, to be able to want all comfort, both human and divine, and to be willing to bear this interior banishment for God's honour, and to seek oneself in nothing, nor to think of one's own merit; therefore when God gives spiritual comfort receive it with thanksgiving, and know that it is the bounty of God. When comforts shall be taken away from thee, do not presently despair, but wait with humility and patience for the heavenly visit, for God is able to restore thee a greater consolation.

"This is no new thing, nor strange, to those who have experienced the ways of God."   S. THOMAS A KEMPIS.

GOD has not promised us that in this world we shall always find comfort in our religion, in so far as comfort means soothing, consolation, satisfaction. "In the world," our dear Master tells us, we "shall have tribulation." It is only when, this life being ended, we wake up in the likeness of Christ, that our souls shall be "satisfied."

But the word comfort implies also the idea of strength, of fortitude, and thus, often when we are unconscious of it, God is comforting us, by giving us strength to endure.

To seek for comfort in the service of God is to seek for

gratification of self, and this He will never give to us on earth. Our life in Christ must be a crucified life, a life of pain, a life of penance, a life bereft of all ease, for if we live with Him, we must also suffer with Him, even unto death.

The love of Jesus must drive out of our hearts all love of self if we would be His disciples. Concerning the things of God, we are not to consider what we like, or even what will do us good. That which our dear Master has appointed for us, we must humbly and patiently do, not looking for, or expecting comfort, but thankful if He lets us find it in our simple obedience to His will.

Let us pray to-day for the same spirit of self-abnegation which made S. Paul ready to suffer the loss of all things for the sake of his brethren.

"Jesus, Lord, be Thou mine own,
Thee I long for, Thee alone;
All myself I give to Thee,
Do whate'er Thou wilt with me.

Thou, O God, my heart inflame,
Give that love which Thou dost claim,
Payment I will ask for none,
Love demands but love alone."

Aspiration.

"*Lord we have left all and followed Thee: what shall we have therefore.*"

Voice of Jesus.

"CANST THOU BE BAPTIZED WITH THE BAPTISM THAT I AM BAPTIZED WITH?"

Read *Psalm cxix. 81 to 88*. Lesson, *Job ii. 7 to 13*.

Litany of the Passion.

First Tuesday in Lent.

PATIENCE.

"O MY GOD, I CRY IN THE DAY-TIME, BUT THOU HEAREST NOT, IN THE NIGHT SEASON ALSO I TAKE NO REST."—PSALM XXII. 2.

"THE GOOD THAT I WOULD I DO NOT: BUT THE EVIL WHICH I WOULD NOT, THAT I DO.

"NOW IF I DO THAT I WOULD NOT, IT IS NO MORE I THAT DO IT, BUT SIN THAT DWELLETH IN ME."—ROMANS VII. 19, 20.

"*Keep thy mind calm and even, and prepare thyself for hearing still more. All is not lost if thou feel thyself often afflicted and grievously tempted.*

"*Thou art man, and not God; thou art flesh, and not an angel. How canst thou think to continue even in the same state of virtue, when this was not found in the angels in Heaven, nor in the first Man in Paradise?*

"*I am He that raises up and saves them that mourn, and them that know their own infirmity I advance to My Divinity.*"

S. THOMAS A KEMPIS.

THE keynote of the harmony of a religious life is patience. It is an attribute of God displayed in all His dealings with men; without it, perseverance and holiness of life are impossible.

Patience must be exercised in three ways; towards ourselves, towards our brethren, and towards God. To-day, we will meditate on the necessity of being patient with ourselves. Our sins and failings are so many, and so great, that they are perpetually hindering us, and driving us away from the strait path in which we desire to walk, and we get angry and impatient with ourselves because of our frequent falls.

The greater the light given to us, and the more sincere our endeavours to walk with God, the greater will be our temptation to be impatient with the follies and infirmities of our sinful nature, which cause us so often to stumble and to fall. This temptation is the more insidious, because it wears the garb of compunction for sin, while it is really only another form of selfishness and pride.

Let us ask God to make us patient, and to teach us to accept our weakness and failures from His hand, as a part of the wholesome penance whereby He will train our souls for Heaven.

> "The Christian soul by patience grows
> More perfect day by day;
> And brighter still and brighter glows,
> With Heaven's eternal ray.
>
> God's goodness made thee what thou art,
> And yet will thee redeem;
> O be thou of a steadfast heart,
> And put thy trust in Him."

Aspiration.
"*Master, carest Thou not that we perish.*"

Voice of Jesus.
"IN YOUR PATIENCE POSSESS YE YOUR SOULS."

Read *Psalm iii.* Lesson, *Romans vii.*

Litany of Patience.

Second Wednesday in Lent.

PATIENCE TOWARDS OUR BRETHREN.

"I SAID IN MY HASTE, ALL MEN ARE LIARS."—PSALM LXXXVI. II.
"WHO MAKETH THEE TO DIFFER FROM ANOTHER? AND WHAT HAST THOU THAT THOU DIDST NOT RECEIVE?"—I COR. IV. 7.

"Son, patience and humility in adversity are more pleasing to Me than much consolation and devotion in prosperity.

"Why art thou disturbed at a little thing said against thee? If it had been more, thou oughtest not to have been moved.

"Thou art valiant enough so long as no adversity or opposition comes in thy way.

"Consider the great frailty which thou often experienced in small difficulties, yet it is intended for thy good, as often as these, or such like things befall thee.

"Put it from thy heart, the best thou canst, and if it has touched thee, yet let it not cast thee down, nor keep thee a long time entangled.

"At least bear it patiently, if thou canst not receive it with joy."

S. THOMAS A KEMPIS.

WORDS that are planted in haste bear the bitter fruit of penitential tears. All the Saints of God, almost without exception, have uttered such words, and have shed for them the tears of penance.

Moses, the meekest of men, forfeited his inheritance in the Land of Promise through an act of impatience. David, the man after God's own heart, said "in haste" that he was cast out of the sight of God, and angrily condemned all his fellow-men, as liars. Job, the most patient of men, turned at last upon his unfeeling friends, and said in his anger, "Miserable comforters are ye all." The Disciple whom Jesus loved, besought Him that he might be allowed to call down fire to destroy the enemies of the Lord, and S. Peter ventured even to rebuke his Holy Master, when He spoke of His coming Passion, saying, "These things be far from Thee, Lord," and thereby called forth the most severe reprimand that was ever uttered by the gracious Lips of Jesus.

But all these Saints died in faith, having repented of their sins, and received the promises of God, and these things are written about them for our learning, that we, through patience, may have hope.

Keep back thy hasty words. Be patient with the brother that offends thee, for thou art weak as he is.

Take heed lest thy angry words cut off thy neighbour's ear, when Christ is not near thee to heal the wound that thou hast made.

May this day's meditation lead us on our way towards the perfect peace of God.

> "Renew Thine Image, Lord, in me,
> Lowly and gentle may I be,
> No charms but these to Thee are dear,
> No anger mayst Thou ever find,
> No pride in my unruffled mind,
> But faith and Heaven-born peace be there.

"A patient and victorious mind,
That life and all things casts behind,
Springs forth obedient to Thy call,
A heart that no desire can move,
But still t' adore, believe, and love,
Give me, my Lord, my Life, my All."

Aspiration.

"*Lord, how often shall my brother sin against me, and I shall forgive him?*"

Voice of Jesus.

"BLESSED ARE THE MEEK, FOR THEY SHALL INHERIT THE EARTH."

Read *Psalm xxxi. 13-27.* Lesson, *Job xix.*

Litany of Patience.

Second Thursday in Lent.

PATIENCE TOWARDS GOD.

"HATH GOD FORGOTTEN TO BE GRACIOUS?"—PSALM LXXVII. 9.

"THE LORD IS NOT SLACK CONCERNING HIS PROMISE, AS SOME MEN COUNT SLACKNESS; BUT IS LONG-SUFFERING TO USWARD, NOT WILLING THAT ANY SHOULD PERISH, BUT THAT ALL SHOULD COME TO REPENTANCE."—2 S. PETER III. 9.

"*Think not thyself wholly forsaken, although for a time I have sent thee some tribulation, or withdrawn from thee the comfort which thou desirest, for this is the way to the Kingdom of Heaven.*

"*I know thy secret thoughts, I know that it is very expedient for thy soul that thou shouldst sometimes be left without consolation lest thou shouldst be puffed up with good success, and shouldst take a complaisance in thyself, imagining thyself to be what thou art not.*

"*I did not send My beloved disciples to temporal joys, but to great conflicts; not to honours, but to contempt; not to idleness but to labours; not to rest, but to bring forth much fruit in patience.*"

S. THOMAS A KEMPIS.

LET us meditate to-day on the patient waiting for God to which He calls all His children, and on which His Benediction rests. It is not easy to learn to wait for God, because we cannot understand His dealings with us, or find out His ways. Therefore, a life of waiting is a life of faith. We cannot wait patiently for that, which we do not believe will in the end, come to us.

A life of waiting is a life of meditation. The thing that we long for, will take up our thoughts and call us away from exterior distractions, to muse on the hidden things of God.

A life of waiting is a life of expectation. If we are waiting for the help and grace of God, we shall ever be looking to Him, and watching for the fulfilment of His promises, fearful lest we should fail to recognize His sweet message when it comes.

The life of waiting is a life of preparation. The more we desire the Presence of the Lord, the more careful we shall be to do nothing which may hinder His coming. We shall endeavour to purify the innermost sanctuary of our hearts, and so to make beautiful the place of His rest. We shall try to make those around us more faithful, more pitiful, more pure.

Let us hold fast our courage and our faith, and be patient to the coming of the Lord. Though He tarry, let us wait patiently for Him, for He will come and will be gracious unto those who look and long for Him.

> "Jesus, my heart's dear Refuge,
> Jesus has died for me,
> Firm on the Rock of Ages
> Ever my trust shall be.
> Here let me wait with patience,
> Wait till the night is o'er;
> Wait till I see the morning
> Break on the golden shore.
> Safe in the arms of Jesus,
> Safe on His gentle breast,
> There by His love o'ershadowed,
> Sweetly my soul shall rest."

Aspiration.
"*How long, O Lord, how long?*"

Voice of Jesus.
"BLESSED ARE THOSE SERVANTS WHOM THE LORD WHEN HE COMETH SHALL FIND WATCHING."

Read *Psalm lxii.* Lesson, *Daniel xii. 5-12.*

Litany of Patience.

Second Friday in Lent.

SUFFERING IN BODY.

"THY LOVING CORRECTION SHALL MAKE ME GREAT."—PSALM XVIII. 35.
"LET IT ALONE THIS YEAR ALSO, TILL I SHALL DIG ABOUT IT."—S. LUKE XIII. 8.

"*Set thyself like a good and faithful servant of Christ to bear manfully the Cross of thy Lord, crucified for the love of thee.*

"*Drink of the chalice of thy Lord lovingly, if thou desirest to be His friend, and to have part with Him.*

"*Leave consolations to God to do with them as best pleaseth Him.*

"*But prepare thyself to bear tribulations, and account them the greatest consolations: for the sufferings of this life bear no proportion with the glory to come, although thou alone couldst suffer them all.*"

S. THOMAS A KEMPIS.

FRIDAY is the day consecrated to the thought of suffering, the day sprinkled for evermore with the Blood of the Great Sacrifice.

Let us then on every Friday keep in our hearts the Feast of the exaltation of the Holy Cross, by lifting up to our Blessed Lord our cross of pain and suffering, and offering it in union with His Sacrifice to the Majesty of God.

Only we must take care that the cross we offer carries on it ourselves. We must be nailed to it before it is lifted up, our wills, our hearts, our intellects must all be fastened there. Then will the Lord, Who for us was lifted up, "draw" us unto Him.

We will bless the cross of pain which raises us nearer to Him Whom we so love. We will gladly bear the suffering, by which our will is fastened to His most Holy Will.

We are trees of the Lord's planting, and He ordains that we should bring forth fruit to His glory. To this end, as a good Husbandman, He prunes and cuts away all withered and useless branches, and He digs deeply, even to the very roots, to loosen the hard soil, and give new strength and nourishment, so that the sap of the grace of God may flow freely even to the topmost branches.

When our vanity and love of ease are cut away by the sharp pruning-knife of bodily pain, and the chastisements of our Father dig deeply to the very roots of our pride and self-will, then let us give praise to God, that He has left us still standing in His holy ground, and that He is making us fit for the Master's use.

> "Inscribed upon the Cross we see,
> In shining letters, God is love;
> He bears our sins upon the Tree,
> He brings us mercy from above.
>
> The Cross it takes our guilt away,
> It holds the fainting spirit up,
> It cheers with hope the gloomy day,
> And sweetens every bitter cup."

Aspiration.
"*Bid me to come unto Thee.*"

Voice of Jesus.
"I, IF I BE LIFTED UP, WILL DRAW ALL MEN UNTO ME."
Read *Psalm cxvi.* Lesson, *Wisdom iii. 1 to 11.*
Litany of the Passion.

Second Saturday in Lent.

QUIETNESS OF MIND.

"HE WATERETH THE HILLS FROM ABOVE, THE EARTH IS FILLED WITH THE FRUIT OF THY WORKS."—PSALM CIV. 13.
"WHICH OF YOU, WITH TAKING THOUGHT, CAN ADD TO HIS STATURE ONE CUBIT."—S. LUKE XII. 26.

"Grant me Thy grace most merciful Jesus, that it may be with me, and continue with me to the end.

"Grant me always to will and desire that which is acceptable to Thee, and which pleaseth Thee best.

"Let Thy will be mine, and let my will always follow Thine, and agree perfectly with it.

"Let me always will or not will the same with Thee: and let me not be able to will or not will any otherwise than as Thou willest or willest not.

"Grant that I may die to all things that are in the world: and for Thy sake, love to be despised, and not to be known in this world.

"Grant that I may rest in Thee above all things desired, and that my heart may be at peace in Thee.

"In this peace, in the self-same that is in Thee, the one Sovereign Eternal Good, I will sleep and I will rest."

S. THOMAS A KEMPIS.

WE will meditate to-day on the quiet working of the grace of God in our hearts.

Our Blessed Lord tells us to consider the lilies how they grow, that we may learn from them. Planted down in the bosom of the earth, in darkness and in silence, unseen and unknown of men, the Hand of God touches them, and draws forth out of that which was apparently dead, new forms of beauty and of life.

As with the lilies, so with the corn. It is sown in faith; unseen by any but the eye of God, its growth begins, and by and bye springs forth, first the blade, then the ear, then the full corn in the ear.

So it is with the children of God. He plants them in His holy ground at their Baptism, and sprinkles them with the Water of Life, and then the gracious Spirit of God begins to work in their hearts in silence, and unseen, till the fulness of the grace He gives, at length breaks forth, and shows the green blade, which is the first token of the coming harvest.

No strife, no hurry, no noise, no rushing hither and thither, but peace, and rest, and quiet waiting for God ; by these shall the sweet lily grow, and attain the full majesty of its pure beauty.

We must beware lest even the religious exercises of the Lenten season should shake our souls from their quietness and peace. With hurry and excitement, self breaks in upon us, and brings the distracting turbulence that draws us away from God.

A great saint has said, "The proficiency of the soul is attained more by loving than by thinking." "Let the body labour, but let the soul rest." By prayer, by meditation, by quiet communing with God, shall the growth of grace within us, be nourished and made strong. The Good Shepherd leads His own sheep beside the still waters. In quietness and in confidence shall be your strength.

Let us learn of the Lily, from whose sweet and lovely flower, nurtured in the silence of the Sanctuary of God, came forth Him, Who was the Desire of the whole earth.

May the words of quiet submission dwell in our hearts this day ; "be it unto me according to Thy Word."

> "Oh ! for a closer walk with God,
> A calm and heavenly frame,
> A light to shine upon the road,
> That leads me to the Lamb.
>
> Give me, dear Lord, a quiet mind,
> From every tumult free,
> A heart endued with patient grace,
> That rests itself on Thee."

> "Give me beneath Thy Cross to lie,
> And fix my gaze on Thee,
> To gain from Thy dear dying Love
> My soul's tranquillity."

Aspiration.
"*Lord, increase our faith.*"

Voice of Jesus.
"LET NOT YOUR HEART BE TROUBLED, NEITHER LET IT BE AFRAID."
Read *Psalm iv.* Lesson, *Isaiah xxx. 15 to 22.*

Litany of the Holy Name of Jesus.

Second Sunday in Lent.

INTERIOR CONSOLATIONS.

"SET UP THYSELF, O GOD, ABOVE THE HEAVENS, AND THY GLORY ABOVE ALL THE EARTH."—PSALM LVII. 12.

"I BESEECH THEE, SHOW US THY GLORY."—EXOD. XXXIII. 18.

" *Every inclination which appears good is not presently to be followed, nor every contrary affection, at first sight, to be rejected.*

"*Even in good desires and inclinations it is expedient sometimes to use some restraint; lest by too much eagerness thou incur distraction of mind; lest thou create scandal to others by not keeping within discipline, or by the opposition which thou mayest meet with from others, thou be suddenly disturbed, and fall.*"   S. THOMAS A KEMPIS.

SUNDAYS should be to us "times of refreshing," days spent in communion with God, days on which we gain strength to bear the trials, and to resist the temptations, incident to the active life of the week.

Second Sunday in Lent. 27

Pre-eminently refreshing to our souls are the Sundays in Lent, when we are relieved from the forty days' fast, and are free to turn our thoughts away from our own inner life, to the contemplation of the glorious Mysteries of our holy Faith.

The Voice of the Church calls us to-day to meditate on the Transfiguration of our Blessed Lord, when He turned aside for a few moments from the bitterness of His earthly life, to manifest to His chosen Apostles a brief glimpse of the glory which He had with the Father before the beginning of the world.

His Divine Countenance was irradiated with heavenly lustre, and His raiment shone white and glistening before the astonished eyes of His Apostles, and on either side of Him appeared the glorified forms of Moses and Elias, talking with Him.

Thus did the dear Master show forth His glory, that His servants might have their faith strengthened, and their hopes renewed, and to this end were they privileged to hear the Voice of God Almighty speaking from the cloud.

God gives to His chosen ones bright visions of His glory for their comfort and their joy, but here on earth such visions cannot last. We must come down from the mountain, and the heavenly visitants must vanish from our sight.

We who have been rejoicing in the worship of the Sanctuary must go back to our everyday trials, and must take up once more the thread of our Lenten discipline.

S. Peter would fain have placed a tabernacle for his Lord in the full radiance of the mountain glory, that he might abide there for ever, but the Scripture tells us "he knew not what he said." The children of God must thankfully receive the joys which their loving Lord gives them, and they must be content to resign them when He takes them away.

"Lord, Thy glory fills the Heaven,
Earth is with its fulness stored,
Unto Thee be glory given,
Holy, Holy, Holy, Lord."

Aspiration.
"*Master, it is good for us to be here.*"

Voice of Jesus.

"FATHER, I WILL THAT THEY ALSO WHOM THOU HAST GIVEN ME, BE WITH ME WHERE I AM."

Read *Psalm cxxxviii.* Lesson, *S. Luke ix. 28 to 37.*

Litany of our Lord Jesus Christ.

Second Monday in Lent.

DIFFICULTIES IN THE WAY.

"I AM SO FAST IN PRISON THAT I CANNOT GET FORTH."—PSALM LXXXVIII. 8.

"THEY CAME UNTO THE IRON GATE THAT LEADETH UNTO THE CITY; WHICH OPENED TO THEM OF HIS OWN ACCORD, AND THEY WENT OUT." ACTS XII. 10.

"*All things avail little till thou take notice that I am He Who delivers those that trust in Me, nor is there out of Me any powerful help.*

"*But now, having recovered spirits after the storm, grow thou strong again in the light of My tender mercies; for I am at hand to repair all, not only to the full, but even with abundance and above measure.*

"*Where is thy faith? Stand firmly, and with perseverance.*

Second Monday in Lent.

"Have patience, be of good courage; comfort will come to thee in its proper season."   S. THOMAS A KEMPIS.

WE have come down from the Mount of Transfiguration. Sunday is past and over.

We must take up our cross afresh, and go bravely forward in the path that is set before us. There are great difficulties in our way, which meet us at once. Our own sins and weaknesses, the opposition of others, feebleness of body—some or all of these form a barrier which we can neither surmount nor remove.

Like S. Peter, we are shut up in prison, chained on the one hand to our sinful bodies, on the other to the temptations and distractions of the world we live in, but let us take courage, and pray without ceasing, and God will help us to "leap over the wall." The iron gate, even which seems to make it impossible for us to follow the guidance of the heavenly messenger shall not oppose us.

We must not waste our time and strength in bewailing the closeness of our captivity. We must not wear out our energies by the constant contemplation of the iron gate of difficulty which bars our road. It is useless to beat ourselves against it, or to try to push it down, its massy bars mock our puny efforts, but rather let us be quiet and pray, putting our case humbly into the Hands of God, and in His good time a light from Heaven will illumine the prison cell, the chains will fall from us, and an angel's voice will bid us arise and go on our way.

If the angel of the Lord be with us, the iron gate will open to us "of his own accord."

"Lord, Thine own Thou wilt deliver,
From the chains of guilt and sin,
Iron bars and strong foundations
Cannot shut Thy children in.

Thou wilt send Thy glorious angel,
From all strife to set them free.
Jesus, ope the Gate of Heaven,
Let Thy children come to Thee."

Aspiration.
"*Jesus, Master, have mercy on us.*"

Voice of Jesus.
"VERILY, VERILY, I SAY UNTO YOU, I AM THE DOOR OF THE SHEEP."

Read *Psalm xviii.* Lesson, *Acts xii. 1 to 12.*

Litany of the Holy Ghost.

Second Tuesday in Lent.

FAULTS OF THE SAINTS.

"WHO WILL LEAD ME INTO THE STRONG CITY?"—PSALM LX. 9.

"THESE THINGS ARE WRITTEN FOR OUR LEARNING, THAT WE THROUGH PATIENCE AND COMFORT OF THE SCRIPTURES MIGHT HAVE HOPE."—ROMANS XV. 4.

"*Turn all occasions to thy spiritual profit; so that if thou seest or hearest any good examples, thou mayest be spurred on to imitate them.*

"*But if thou observe anything that is blameworthy, take heed that thou commit not the same, or if thou at any time hast done it, labour to amend it out of hand.*

"*A religious man, who exercises himself seriously and devoutly in the most Holy Life and Passion of our Lord, shall find there abundantly all things profitable and necessary for him; nor need he seek any better model than that of Jesus."*   S. THOMAS A KEMPIS.

EVEN the faults of the Saints, which have been recorded by the inspiration of the Holy Ghost, ought to be to us a source of consolation. We regard the holy men of old as those whom we must follow, but only at a distance, and without any hope of attaining to the height of their sanctity. But the command of God is "Be ye perfect," and nothing short of perfection must satisfy those who try to walk with God.

Yet we are so imperfect. We cannot do anything really well. Year after year we use all the blessed means of grace, we live in constant nearness to the sweet mysteries of our holy Faith, and still we remain almost as we were.

Again and again we have the same sins to confess, the same infirmities keep us back, the same weaknesses cause us to fall.

Praised be God! This is true also of the greatest of His Saints. Although the grace of God abounded in them, and made them so powerful to do Him service, yet the special characteristics of each remained unchanged.

S. Peter, hasty before his call, remained rash and impetuous after; S. John, zealous and loving always, allowed the fervour of his devotion to carry him away from the meekness which his Divine Master taught him; S. Thomas, too practical and too weak in faith, needed to the last to walk by sight, and to have sensible assurance of the truth of the Resurrection.

These faults of the Saints are written that we may have hope.

If S. Peter and S. John could mistake the Spirit of the dear Master's teaching, even while He was with them on earth, is it wonderful that we too should sometimes allow enthusiasm or zeal, or even a too practical spirit of common sense, to overpower us, and bring down upon us the rebuke of our God.

But while He rebukes, He holds out His pierced Hands, and draws us with the cords of love close to His wounded Heart, so have we a good hope because of His Word.

> "For Christ they lived, for Christ they died,
> Him in their lives they crucified,
> Their death their greatest gain.
> Now in the mansions of the blest,
> With Him in blissful peace they rest,
> Awaiting the Last Day.
> Like them, may we our labour love,
> And faithful to His service prove,
> Till we are called away."

Aspiration.
"Thou hast the words of Eternal Life."

Voice of Jesus.
"BE YE THEREFORE PERFECT, AS YOUR FATHER WHICH IS IN HEAVEN IS PERFECT."

Read *Psalm lxi.* Lesson, *Heb. xii. to verse 14.*

Litany of the Holy Ghost.

Third Wednesday in Lent.

WARFARE.

"THEY THAT ARE MINE ENEMIES AND WOULD DESTROY ME GUILTLESS ARE MIGHTY."—PSALM LXIX. 4.

"THERE WAS WAR IN HEAVEN."—REV. XXI. 7.

" *Son, thou art more serene in this life; but as long as thou livest, thou hast need always of spiritual arms.*

" *Thou art in the midst of enemies, and art assaulted on all sides.*

" *If thou dost not fix thy heart on Me, with a sincere will of suffering all things for My sake, thou canst not support the heat of this warfare, nor attain to the victory of the Saints. It behoveth thee, therefore, to go through all manfully, and to use a strong hand against all things that oppose thee.*"

S. THOMAS A KEMPIS.

THE angels sang of "Peace on earth" when the Saviour of the world was born, but when He came to man's estate, He told His disciples that He was not come to bring peace, but division. Yet again He said, " Peace I leave with you, My peace I give unto you." How can these things be?

God calls us to fight against His enemies, but to be at peace with Him.

If God be for us, we need not fear those who are against us.

All our life may be, and ought to be, one continued time of warfare against our threefold enemy, the Devil, the World, and the Flesh. But while the battle rages never so fiercely, God gives to His children a sweet sense of nearness to His Ineffable Majesty, which fills their souls with peace.

While we fight on the Lord's side, our victory, too, is sure. Only we must take heed lest haply we be fighting under the standard of pride and self-love, for such a warfare God will not bless.

Let us fix our eyes steadfastly on the Banner which goes before us. If it bear the Sign of the Cross, we may follow it fearlessly, and we shall at last receive from the dear Master's own Hand, the crown which He has promised to him that overcometh in the strife.

"The Royal Banners forward go,
The Cross shines forth in mystic glow,
When He in Flesh, our flesh Who made,
Our sentence bore, our ransom paid.

Fulfilled is all that David told,
In true prophetic song of old.
Amidst the nations, 'God,' saith he,
' Hath reigned, and triumphed from the Tree.'"

Aspiration.

"Blessed be the King that cometh in the Name of the Lord; peace in Heaven and Glory in the Highest."

Voice of Jesus.

"SUPPOSE YE THAT I AM COME TO GIVE PEACE ON EARTH, I TELL YOU, NAY."

Read *Psalm xxxv.* Lesson, *Eph. vi. 2 to 12.*

Litany of the Holy Name of Jesus.

Third Thursday in Lent.

FOES WITHIN.

"CLEANSE THOU ME FROM MY SECRET FAULTS."—PSALM XIV. 10.

"JUDGE NOTHING BEFORE THE TIME, UNTIL THE LORD COME, WHO BOTH WILL BRING TO LIGHT THE HIDDEN THINGS OF DARKNESS, AND WILL MAKE MANIFEST THE COUNSELS OF THE HEARTS: AND THEN SHALL EVERY MAN HAVE PRAISE OF GOD."—1 COR. IV. 5.

"*O Lord, my God, depart not far from me, O my God, have regard to help me; for divers evil thoughts have risen up against me, and great fears afflicting my soul.*

"*How shall I pass without hurt? How shall I break through them?*

"*Thou sayest 'I will open the gates of the prison, and reveal to thee hidden secrets.'*

"*Do, Lord, as thou sayest, and let all these wicked thoughts flee from before Thy Face.*" S. THOMAS A KEMPIS.

IT is not from the enemies in the field, nor even from those at the gate, that the besieged fortress has most to fear. Its greatest danger lies in the possibility of treachery within the walls.

If there be but one unfaithful guard who will open the smallest aperture, the strong defences and the most careful strategy are of no avail whatever. Through the one unguarded window the hosts of the enemy will pour in like a flood, and the fortress will fall a prey to the fury of the oppressors.

We will meditate to-day on the danger of those secret sins which are the treacherous guards of the stronghold of our souls. They are often unknown to us, and yet they are the most formidable and dangerous of all our foes.

How are we to discover and defeat them?

By self-examination, by meditation, and by prayer, through the help of the Holy Spirit of God.

If we let into the darkest recesses of our souls the glorious light of the Gospel of Christ, it will reveal clearly to us all the dark thoughts and secret sins which are lurking there. When once they are discovered and brought into the light, their treachery is disarmed, and we need fear them no more.

To meditate on the life and character of our Blessed Lord, and to pray for the same mind to be in us which we see in Him, this will bring to light the hidden things of darkness, and conquer the dominion of secret sin.

So shall our souls rejoice and praise with a pure heart the God of Peace.

"Light of those whose dreary dwelling
Borders on the shades of night,
Come, and by Thy love dispelling
Dissipate the clouds beneath.

By Thine All-restoring Spirit
Every burdened soul release,
Every weary, wand'ring spirit,
Guide Thou into perfect peace."

Aspiration.

"*Lord, that I may receive my sight.*"

Voice of Jesus.

"FOR JUDGMENT AM I COME INTO THIS WORLD, THAT THEY WHO SEE NOT MIGHT SEE."

Read *Psalm cxxxix.* Lesson, *S. John iii. 16-22.*

Litany of Repentance.

Third Friday in Lent.

SUFFERING OF MIND.

"MY TEARS HAVE BEEN MY MEAT DAY AND NIGHT, WHILE THEY SAY DAILY UNTO ME, 'WHERE IS NOW THY GOD.'"—PSALM XLII. 3.
" BEHOLD WE COUNT THEM HAPPY WHO ENDURE."—S. JAMES V. II.

" Know for certain that thou must lead a dying life; and the more a man dies to himself, the more he begins to live to God.

" No man is fit to comprehend heavenly things who has not resigned himself to suffer for Christ.

" Nothing is more acceptable to God, nothing more wholesome for thee in this world, than to suffer willingly for Christ."

S. THOMAS A KEMPIS.

ONCE more Friday brings us to the Feet of Him Who was "lifted up that He might draw all things unto Him."

Let us come then to the Cross of Jesus, and lay down there the burden of sorrow, which, all unknown to our brethren and companions, weighs down in a greater or less degree the heart of every true servant of the Lord.

The Divine Master tells us plainly that if we would be His, tribulation must be our portion here. He was the "Man of Sorrows," and shall not the disciple be "as his Master?"

While we are on earth we must bear the grief of our own sins, we must also mourn over the wickedness of the world around, and the dishonour which is being done to God by the creatures of His Hand, and we have each of us a secret burden of bitterness to carry, known only to our own aching hearts.

Only let us pray that Jesus will draw us in our sorrow unto Himself. The bitterest of all woe is the feeling of separation from God.

We know that He will never really leave us or forsake us, but there are times when in our tribulation we cannot see Him, when we "feel after" Him in our darkness, and cannot find Him.

Then indeed our burden seems to be too heavy for us to bear, but let us lift up our heads and look on Him Whom they pierced, and we shall find comfort, for we shall see God in the Face of Jesus Christ.

> "The while I fain would tread the heavenly way,
> Evil is present with me day by day,
> Yet in mine ears the gracious tidings fall,
> Repent, believe, confess, thou shalt be free from all.
>
> It is the voice of Jesus that I hear,
> His are the Hands stretched out to draw me near,
> And His the Blood that can for all atone,
> And set me faultless there before the throne."

Aspiration.
"Lord, we know not whither Thou goest."

Voice of Jesus.
"IF I GO NOT AWAY THE COMFORTER WILL NOT COME UNTO YOU."

Read *Psalm xiv.* Lesson, *Isa. liii.*

Litany of the Passion.

Third Saturday in Lent.

OBEDIENCE.

"THOU ART MY PORTION, O LORD, I HAVE PROMISED TO KEEP THY LAW."—PSALM CXIX. 57.

"TO OBEY IS BETTER THAN SACRIFICE."—I SAM. XV. 22.

" In regard to that little of thy will, which thou now willingly forsakest, thou shalt for ever have thy will in Heaven.

" There thy will, being always one with Mine, shall desire nothing foreign.

" There I will give thee a garment of praise for thy sorrow.

" There will the fruit of obedience appear, and humble subjection shall be gloriously crowned."   *S. THOMAS A KEMPIS.*

SATURDAY is the Sabbath of old, "Creation's day of rest," a rest from the toils and warfare of the week, a time of preparation for the holy functions of the Great First Day on which Jesus rose, victorious over sin and death.

Therefore our Saturday meditation ought to partake of the character both of rest, and of preparation.

To some people these are antagonistic terms : to them preparation involves bustle, and hurry, and agitation ; they only look for rest when that for which they have prepared is come.

But Jesus says, "Take My yoke upon you, and learn of Me, and ye shall find rest."

The soul's true rest is in obedience to the law of Christ, and by this obedience only can it be prepared for its inheritance among the Saints.

Obedience is the first step on the angelic ladder which leads from earth to Heaven ; it is the first act of our Holy

Faith which children learn; it is the chariot of fire by which the aged Saint ascends to the Mount of God. It is the brightest jewel in the martyr's glorious crown.

Obedience involves the other holy virtues of Faith, and Love, and confidence in God.

Its exercise gives us strength in adversity, and sanctifies our times of joy. It brings down the high looks of the proud, and nourishes in us the childlike spirit, which Jesus loves so well.

Above all, it makes us like to our Blessed Lord and Master. From the supernal glory of His eternal reign in the Kingdom of His Father, His voice of submission sounds forth, "I come to do Thy Will, O My God."

His life on earth was throughout a life of obedience, in the holy home of Nazareth, in His ministry in the "form of a servant," above all on Calvary, where by His death He consummated the last dread act of obedience which the justice of God requires from those He has created. "He became obedient unto death, even the death of the Cross."

> "Fear Him, ye Saints, and you will then
> Have nothing else to fear,
> Make you His service your delight,
> Your wants shall be His care."

Aspiration.
"*Abide with us.*"

Voice of Jesus.
"YE ARE MY FRIENDS IF YE DO WHATEVER I COMMAND YE."

Read *Psalm cxix. 33 to 41.* Lesson, *S. Matt. xviii. 1-12.*

Litany of the Holy Name of Jesus.

Third Sunday in Lent.

LIGHT.

"GOD HATH SHOWED US LIGHT, BIND THE SACRIFICE WITH CORDS, YEA, EVEN TO THE HORNS OF THE ALTAR."—PSALM CXVIII. 27.

"IN HIM IS NO DARKNESS AT ALL."—1 S. JOHN I. 5.

"*Enlighten me, O good Jesus, with the brightness of eternal light, and cast out all darkness from the dwelling of my heart.*

"*Restrain my many wandering thoughts, and suppress the temptations that assault me.*

"*Fight strongly for me, that peace may be made in Thy power, and the abundance of Thy praise may resound in Thy holy court, which is a clean conscience.*

"*Send forth Thy Light and Thy Truth that they may shine upon the earth; for I am as earth that is empty and void, till Thou enlightenest me.*" S. THOMAS A KEMPIS.

To-day begins the last week of the first part of our Lenten meditations, the part which treats of ourselves, and of our "death unto sin."

This last week we will devote to the consideration of those things which hold us back from God, that so by His blessing we may seem to clear out of our way all that opposes itself and hinders our progress, and with calm and devout minds, give ourselves to earnest meditation on our new life in Christ, till our longings and aspirations mark their climax in the surpassing joy of Easter Day.

We begin this week then, as the Church suggests by the words of the Epistle, by a few thoughts about light.

We have seen that it is Jesus Who is the Light of the world, and that in His Light we both see what are our sins, and also are we able to trace the exceeding greatness of the love and mercy of God, which He has revealed to us.

Let us now consider the call of God that we should walk in the Light which He has given. That call involves the sacrifice of all in us that shrinks from light, and would fain hide itself when the voice of God is heard among the trees of our garden.

We must "walk as children of light."

As children of light we must walk in love, following our Divine Master, we must reprove the works of darkness, we must arise and shine before men, not with any lustre of our own, but with the reflected radiance of the brightness of Him Who has called us to holiness, as His "dear children."

> "Thy lovely Presence shines so clear
> Through every sense and way,
> That souls which once have seen Thee dear
> See all things else decay.
>
> Come Thou, dear Lord, possess my heart,
> Chase thence the shades of night,
> Come, pierce it with Thy piercing dart,
> And ever-shining light."

Aspiration.
"*Lord, to whom shall we go?*"

Voice of Jesus.
"I AM THE WAY, THE TRUTH, AND THE LIFE."

Read *Psalm cxii.* Lesson, *Eph. v.*

Litany of the Holy Ghost.

Third Monday in Lent.

WHAT HOLDS US BACK?

"I WILL WALK AT LIBERTY FOR I SEEK THY COMMANDMENTS."—PSALM CXIX. 8.

"YE WILL NOT COME TO ME THAT YE MIGHT HAVE LIFE."—S. JOHN V. 40.

"*They that love Jesus for Jesus' sake, and not for any comfort of their own, bless Him no less in tribulation and anguish of heart than in the greatest consolation. And if He should never give them His comfort, yet would they always praise Him, and give Him thanks.*

"*Oh! how much is the pure love of Jesus able to do when it is not mixed with any self-interest or self-love!*"   S. THOMAS A KEMPIS.

IN the course of these, our Lenten meditations, we have seen the deceitfulness of sin, and our own helplessness and frailty. We have seen also, have we not! how gracious the Lord is, how full of compassion and mercy. Why do we hesitate then to cast in our lot with Him? Why are we not ready to suffer the loss of all things if only we may win Christ, and be found in Him? What is it that makes us cold to Him, and deaf to the summons of His tender Voice, when He calls His sheep by name? What is it which holds us back from Him?

In one word we may answer, self.

It is that human nature of ours which our dear Lord has condescended to make His own, and to raise to the highest realms of glory, which drags us down, and holds us back, and binds us with chains of iron, lest we should use our liberty as children of God.

Jesus bore our human nature that He might teach us how it can be sanctified, and glorified, and moulded to the Will of God, by the holy discipline of suffering.

The self that holds us back from Jesus must be nailed to the Cross with Him, and every thought of our hearts must be brought into captivity to the Law of Christ, before we can rejoice in the liberty, wherewith He will make us free.

When self, with its sinful affections and lusts, is dead, then our new life in Christ will begin ; the heaviness that has darkened our lives will give place to a morning of joy. We shall then have a "free heart" to offer to the Lord, Whom we love, and His service shall be the delight of our souls.

> " Lead, kindly Light, amid th' encircling gloom,
>   Lead Thou me on ;
> The night is dark, and I am far from home,
>   Lead Thou me on.
> Keep Thou my feet ; I do not ask to see
> The distant scene ; one step enough for me.
>
> So long Thy power hath blessed me, sure it still
>   Will lead me on
> O'er moor and fen, o'er crag and torrent, till
>   The night is gone,
> And with the morn those angel faces smile,
> Which I have loved long since, and lost awhile."

Aspiration.
"*Lord, why cannot I follow Thee now ?*"

Voice of Jesus.
"FOLLOW ME, AND LET THE DEAD BURY THEIR DEAD."

Read *Psalm xc.* Lesson, *S. Matt. x. 16-34.*

Litany of Penitence.

Third Tuesday in Lent.

SELF-WILL.

"I WILL RUN THE WAY OF THY COMMANDMENTS WHEN THOU HAST SET MY HEART AT LIBERTY."—PSALM CXIX. 32.
"NOT WHAT I WILL, BUT AS THOU WILT."—S. MARK XIV. 36.

" He who strives to withdraw himself from obedience, withdraws himself from grace.

" If a man doth not freely and willingly submit himself, it is a sign that his flesh is not as yet perfectly obedient to him, but oftentimes rebels and murmurs.

" There is no more troublesome or worse enemy to the soul than thou art thyself, when not agreeing well with the spirit. Thou must in good earnest conceive a true contempt of thyself, if thou wilt prevail over flesh and blood.

" Learn to break thy own will, and to yield thyself up to all subjection."
                                            S. THOMAS A KEMPIS.

How can we dare to say to Him that formed us, Why hast Thou made me thus? Who are we that we should resist the mighty will of Him by Whom all things consist? Yet it is true that our self-will is the most powerful chain that holds us down to earth, and prevents our following our Blessed Master along the way of the Cross.

To resist control is the earliest effort of the childish mind, the love of independence grows with our growth, and if unchecked by the grace of the Holy Spirit of God, it takes the place of God, and self becomes the one object of our veneration and our love.

Therefore has our dear Lord in mercy ordained that we should be under obedience even in our daily life on earth.

Children to parents, wives to husbands, servants to masters, workers to those who employ them, the whole nation to him who rules over it, that all may, in the ordinary routine of their calling, learn the precious lesson of submission.

The same law rules the Church of God. No man liveth to himself, neither must any do what is right in his own eyes, but all, both those who govern, and those who are under them, must be in subjection to the Law of Christ.

We do not know what is good for us, we cannot look into the future and see what will be required of us; we do not even know what we should pray for, or how to pray aright.

Let then our one most constant prayer be that which hallowed the Garden of Gethsemane. "Not my will, O Lord, but Thine be done."

"Thine Image, Lord, bestow,
    Thy Presence and Thy Love;
I ask to serve Thee here below,
    And reign with Thee above.

Teach me to live by faith,
    Conform my will to Thine;
Let me victorious be in death,
    And then in glory shine."

Aspiration.
"*Thou hast the words of Eternal Life.*"

Voice of Jesus.
"I SEEK NOT MINE OWN WILL, BUT THE WILL OF THE FATHER WHICH HATH SENT ME."

Read *Psalm cxliii*. Lesson, *Romans xv. 1 to 8*.

Litany of Repentance.

Fourth Wednesday in Lent.

SELF-LOVE.

"NOT UNTO US, O LORD, NOT UNTO US, BUT UNTO THY NAME GIVE THE PRAISE."—PSALM CXV. 1.

"YE SHALL BE HATED OF ALL MEN FOR MY NAME'S SAKE."—S. LUKE XXI. 17.

" I became the most humble and most abject of all Men, that thou mightest learn to overcome thy pride by My humility.

" Mine Eye hath spared thee because thy soul was precious in My sight, that thou mightest know My Love, and mightest be always thankful for My favour, and that thou mightest give thyself continually to true subjection and humility."   S. THOMAS A KEMPIS.

THERE are those who, like S. Paul, lament over the weakness of their flesh, who carry on a perpetual warfare against the law of evil, which exists in their sinful nature, but such as these are not held back in their Christian course by self-love.

Self-love is the parent of self-will. It feeds and nourishes it, and does mortal harm to the soul which falls under its dominion.

Self-love inspires us with confidence in ourselves, it tries to silence the voice of conscience, by instigating pride and satisfaction in our own achievements, it is ever sounding our own praises in our ears, and thus it makes us deaf to the gracious Voice of our dear Lord, when He calls us to deny ourselves, and to go and follow Him.

Self-love fills our hearts with thoughts and anxieties about our own pains and troubles and difficulties, and so makes us blind to the needs and sorrows of those to whom God calls us to minister. Hence our selfishness robs us of the soul-inspiring grace of charity.

If we love self, we cannot love either God or our neighbour according to the commandment of Christ.

If our love be cold, we cannot render to God an acceptable service, we cannot praise Him with a thankful heart, we cannot pour out our soul before Him in prayer, we cannot give to others the comfort " wherewith we ourselves are comforted of God."

Let us watch and pray, then, against this weapon of self-love, wherewith the spirit of evil so sorely wounds our souls.

The only cure for such hurt lies in the thought of God.

If we meditate on Him as "our Father;" revealed to us in His Son, Who is also the Son of Man; if we trace His infinite perfections in all His works and ways; we shall learn in the light of His marvellous beauty, to see our own sinfulness, and, like holy Job, to abhor ourselves, and to sit in dust and ashes, mourning and lamenting over the sins which have held us back from God.

> " In vain we tune our formal songs,
> In vain we strive to rise,
> Hosannas languish on our tongues,
> And our devotion dies.
>
> Dear Lord, and shall we ever live
> At this poor dying rate?
> Our love so faint, so cold to Thee,
> And Thine to us so great."

Fourth Thursday in Lent.

Aspiration.
"*Master, which is the first and great commandment in the Law?*"

Voice of Jesus.
"THOU SHALT LOVE THE LORD THY GOD, AND HIM ONLY SHALT THOU SERVE."

Read *Psalm xciv.* Lesson, *1 John iii. 1-14.*

Litany of our Lord Jesus Christ.

Fourth Thursday in Lent.

SELF-INDULGENCE.

"I SAID, I WILL TAKE HEED UNTO MY WAYS."—PSALM XXXIX. 1.

"THE FOXES HAVE HOLES, AND THE BIRDS OF THE AIR HAVE NESTS, BUT THE SON OF MAN HATH NOT WHERE TO LAY HIS HEAD."—S. LUKE IX. 58.

"*It is not the obtaining or multiplying things externally that avails thee, but rather the despising of them, and cutting them up by the root out of thy heart; which I would not have thee to understand only with regard to money and riches, but also with regard to the ambition of honour, and the desire of empty praise, all which things pass away with the world.*

"*The place avails little if the spirit of fervour be wanting, neither shall that peace stand long which is sought from abroad, if the state of thy heart wants the true foundation; that is, if thou stand not in Me.*"

S. THOMAS A KEMPIS.

SELF-INDULGENCE is the laying down of the Cross which our Lord has told us to take up and carry after Him; it is the pampering and indulging of that flesh which our Divine Master has told us to crucify; it is the cherishing an affection for the things of this world, of which He says, "If any man love the world, the love of the Father is not in him."

To indulge self is to follow the lust of the flesh, the lust of the eyes, and the pride of life, which things shall bring the soul to ruin and to death.

Let us then meditate to-day on the necessity which is laid on the servants of Christ, to mortify the flesh, with all that belongs to it, not because of any merit in the act of mortification, but because we long to be like our dear Lord, and to break every chain which holds us back from Him.

There is only one road which leads to Eternal Life, and that is the "Way of the Cross." If we choose that road, and follow it manfully, withdrawing our eyes and ears, and even our thoughts, from all that may seduce us into other paths, we shall find peace, even though the way be long and dreary, and our feet are bruised and bleeding as we go; but if we refuse to follow this strait and narrow way, if we allow ourselves to be led by silken ropes into the broad smooth highway of indolence and ease, God in His mercy will send His storms and tempests upon us, to check our downward course, and to drive us for shelter to the shadow of the Cross.

Therefore, let us rejoice and thank God when He lays His chastening Hand upon us, to rouse us from our fatal sleep, let us grasp His merciful Hand, even though it smite us, and clinging to Him, let us pray that He will lead us back to the way of the Cross again, and will point out to us the traces of the bleeding footsteps of Him, Who "trod the winepress alone," our Master and our God.

> "Lovest thou praise? the Cross is shame;
> Or ease? the Cross is bitter grief;
> More pangs than heart or tongue can frame,
> Men suffered there without relief.
>
> The wanderer seeks his native bower,
> And we will look and long for Thee,
> And thank Thee for each trying hour,
> Wishing, not struggling, to be free."

Aspiration.
"Lord, what shall I do that I may work the works of God?"

Voice of Jesus.
"WHOSOEVER WILL SAVE HIS LIFE SHALL LOSE IT; BUT WHOSOEVER WILL LOSE HIS LIFE FOR MY SAKE, THE SAME SHALL SAVE IT."

Read *Psalm cxix. 65-73.* Lesson, *Romans xiii.*

Litany of Repentance.

Fourth Friday in Lent.

FAITHFULNESS OF GOD.

"I KNOW, O LORD, THAT THY JUDGMENTS ARE RIGHT: AND THAT THOU OF VERY FAITHFULNESS HAST CAUSED ME TO BE TROUBLED."—PSALM CXIX. 75.

"WHEREFORE, LET THEM THAT SUFFER ACCORDING TO THE WILL OF GOD COMMIT THE KEEPING OF THEIR SOULS TO HIM IN WELL-DOING, AS UNTO A FAITHFUL CREATOR."—2 PETER IV. 19.

> "*The sign of the Cross shall be in Heaven, when the Lord shall come to judge.*
>
> "*Then all the servants of the Cross, who in their life-time have conformed themselves to Him that was crucified, shall come to Christ their Judge with great confidence. There is no health of the soul nor hope of Eternal Life but in the Cross. God would have thee learn to suffer tribulation without comfort, and wholly to submit thyself to Him, and to become more humble by tribulation.*"
>
> S. THOMAS A KEMPIS.

As we approach to-day the Foot of the Holy Cross, let it point to the Faithfulness of God, as the subject for our prayerful thought. God has revealed to us what is His Will concerning each of us. It is that we should be sanctified, be made holy and clean, and fit for the Master's use here on earth, and so be fitted and prepared to wear the white robes of the redeemed in Heaven.

"This is the Will of God, even our sanctification," and to this end He orders all the events of our lives, as a Faithful and Wise Creator, Who sees what discipline is necessary to mould us to conformity with His Will.

It is through suffering only that this mortal can put on immortality. It is with pain and much affliction that the image of the earthly can be transformed into the image of the heavenly.

Therefore, let us not fret and complain when our Heavenly Father lays His chastening Hand upon us. Let us rather rejoice that He, in His Faithfulness, has caused us to be troubled, and let us thankfully commend the keeping of our souls to Him.

It is His Will that we should be saved, it is His Will that we should be made perfect, it is His Will that we

Fourth Saturday in Lent.

should follow our Blessed Lord, and be made like unto Him. The only way of sanctification, the only way of perfection is the way of the Cross.

Faithful is He Who has called us to follow it.

> "Take, my soul, thy full salvation,
>   Rise o'er sin, and fear, and care;
> Joy to find in every station
>   Something still to do or bear.
> Think what Spirit dwells within thee,
>   What a Father's smile is thine,
> What a Saviour died to win thee,
>   Child of Heaven dost thou repine?
>
> Hasten on from grace to glory,
>   Armed by faith and winged by prayer,
> Heaven's eternal day's before thee,
>   God's own Hand shall guide thee there."

Aspiration.
"*Lord Jesus, receive my spirit.*"

Voice of Jesus.
"I HAVE PRAYED FOR THEE THAT THY FAITH FAIL NOT."

Read *Psalm cxix. 73-81.* Lesson, *2 Thess. iii. 1 to 14.*

Litany of the Passion.

Fourth Saturday in Lent.

FEAR.

"O KNIT MY HEART UNTO THEE, THAT I MAY FEAR THY NAME." PSALM LXXXVI. 2.

"PERFECT LOVE CASTETH OUT FEAR."—1 S. JOHN IV. 18.

> "*If in the angels Thou hast found sin, and hast not spared them, what will become of me?*
>
> "*Stars have fallen from Heaven, and I, that am but dust, how can I presume?*
>
> "*There is, then, no sanctity if Thou, O Lord, withdraw Thy Hand. No wisdom avails if Thou cease to govern us.*
>
> "*No strength is of any help if Thou support us not.*
>
> "*For if we are left to ourselves we sink and we perish; but if Thou visit us we are raised up, and we live.*
>
> "*Fear God, and thou shalt have no need of being afraid of man.*
>
> "*See thou have God before thine eyes, and do not contend with complaining words.*"   S. THOMAS A KEMPIS.

THE fear of the Lord is the beginning of wisdom. The first lesson we learn of the wisdom and knowledge of God is His exceeding awfulness and the terror of His judgments. When it is first revealed to us Who and what the Omnipotent God is, in His works and in His Word, our soul is filled with fear of Him, because as soon as His Light shines into our souls it shews us our unworthiness and our sinfulness in His Sight. We learn to know God first as a Righteous Judge, and for fear of Him we begin to try to make our lives conformable to His Will.

But when we come to know God in the Person of His Divine Son, then we cease to fear Him as a dread and severe Judge, and we learn instead, to look to Him with the reverence and godly fear wherewith dutiful children look to their Father. When we learn the exceeding great love of God towards us, as it is manifested in the life and death of our Most Blessed Lord and Master, we feel that we cannot do half enough to shew our love to Him, and the dread of

His judgments has changed to fear lest our own sin and weakness should hold us back from entire devotion to His service.

See how this " godly fear" will sanctify our lives; how it will govern our understanding, conforming all our studies to the mind of Christ; how it will foster in us the sweet grace of humility, without which we can render no acceptable service to God; how it will raise the intention and direction of our whole lives into a constant waiting for Christ and looking up to Him; how it will purify and sanctify our daily intercourse with each other when they who fear the Lord speak often to one another in the ears of Him Who dwelleth in the Heavens; how it will remove from the faithful ones all the carking cares and anxieties of life, for we read that though "the lions may lack and suffer hunger, they that fear the Lord shall want no manner of thing that is good."

> " I love to kiss each print where Thou
>   Hast set Thine unseen Feet;
> I cannot fear Thee, Will of God,
>   Thine Empire is so sweet.
>
> I have no cares, O Blessed Will,
>   For all my cares are Thine;
> I live in triumph, Lord, for Thou
>   Hast made Thy triumphs mine.
>
> Man's weakness waiting upon God
>   Its end can never miss,
> For men on earth no work can do
>   More angel-like than this."

Aspiration.
"My soul doth magnify the Lord."

Voice of Jesus.
"FEAR NOT, LITTLE FLOCK, FOR IT IS YOUR FATHER'S GOOD PLEASURE TO GIVE YOU THE KINGDOM."

Read *Psalm lxvi.* Lesson, *Malachi iii. 8 to 18.*

Litany of the Holy Ghost.

END OF PART I.

PART II.

Living Unto Christ.

Fourth Sunday in Lent.

REFRESHMENT.

"MY SONG SHALL BE OF MERCY AND JUDGMENT; UNTO THEE, O LORD, WILL I SING."—PSALM CI. I.

"REPENT YE, THEREFORE, AND BE CONVERTED, THAT YOUR SINS MAY BE BLOTTED OUT WHEN THE TIMES OF REFRESHING SHALL COME FROM THE PRESENCE OF THE LORD."—ACTS III. 7.

"Above all things, and in all things, do thou, my soul, rest always in the Lord, for He is the Eternal Rest of the Saints.

"Give me, O most sweet and loving Jesus, to repose in Thee above all things created, above all health and beauty, above all power and dignity, above all knowledge and subtlety, above all riches and arts, above all joy and gladness, above all fame and praise, above all sweetness and consolation, above all hope and promise, above all merit and desire, above all the gifts and presents that Thou canst give and impart, above all the joy and jubilation that the mind can contain and experience; in fine, above all angels and archangels, and all the hosts of Heaven; above all things visible and invisible, and above all that which is less than Thee, my God.

"For Thou, O Lord my God, art the best above all things; Thou alone most High; Thou alone most Powerful; Thou alone most sufficient and most full; Thou alone most sweet and most full of consolation."

S. THOMAS A KEMPIS.

WE have now reached Mid-Lent Sunday, "Refreshment Sunday," as it is called. May it be to us all a day of strengthening and refreshing, a day on which we gather new courage and energy to continue our Christian course, a day on which our hearts dwell with grateful love and praise on all that Jesus has done for the souls and bodies of men.

Let us take as our special thought for to-day the words from the Epistle, "Jerusalem which is above is free."

Nothing can be more refreshing to our souls than to meditate on the beautiful City of Peace which God has prepared to be the home of His faithful children.

Here we have no "continuing city," we are always obliged to be journeying on, plodding and toiling along weary roads, and bound with many a galling chain to the things of earth when our spirits long to rise and meet their Lord.

But Jerusalem which is above is free, and she is the mother of us all. In her shall every longing of the soul be satisfied, on her breast shall every trouble be soothed to rest, and the only bondage which will rule us in her will be the dominion of love; so shall we dwell for ever in the peace of God, and rejoice in the liberty wherewith Christ has made us free.

Even while we are here on earth we can hear the songs of that land of joy; let us then attune our hearts to listen to them; even here in the house of our pilgrimage, the Good Shepherd feeds us beside still waters; let us then rejoice in Him, and carefully gather together every fragment which remains of His Feasts of Refreshment, that nothing which His gracious Hand bestows may be thrown away by us or lost.

> "Oh! heavenly Jerusalem,
> Eternal are thy halls,
> And blessed are the chosen ones
> That dwell within thy walls.

"Thou art the golden home of peace,
Where Saints for ever sing,
The seat of God's own heritage,
The Palace of the King."

Aspiration.
"*Show us the Father, and it sufficeth us.*"

Voice of Jesus.
"MY PEACE I GIVE UNTO YOU, NOT AS THE WORLD GIVETH, GIVE I UNTO YOU."

Read *Psalm cxlvii.* Lesson, *Rev. xxi. 1 to 8.*

Litany of Jesus Christ.

Fourth Monday in Lent.

SIMPLICITY.

"BEHOLD, EVEN AS THE EYES OF SERVANTS LOOK UNTO THE HAND OF THEIR MASTERS, AND AS THE EYES OF A MAIDEN UNTO THE HAND OF HER MISTRESS: EVEN SO OUR EYES WAIT UPON THE LORD OUR GOD, UNTIL HE HAVE MERCY UPON US."—PSALM CXXIII. 2.

"BUT I FEAR LEST BY ANY MEANS, AS THE SERPENT BEGUILED EVE THROUGH HIS SUBTLETY, SO YOUR MINDS SHOULD BE CORRUPTED FROM THE SIMPLICITY THAT IS IN CHRIST."—2 COR. XI. 3.

"*Who is the man that is able to keep himself so warily, and with so much circumspection in all things, as not to fall sometimes into some deceit or perplexity?*

"*But he that trusts in Thee, O Lord, and seeks Thee with a simple heart, does not so easily fall.*

"*How secure it is for the keeping of heavenly grace to fly the sight of men, and not seek those things that seem to cause admiration abroad, but with all diligence to follow that which brings amendment of life and fervour.*

Fourth Monday in Lent.

"Nature is crafty, and draws away many; ensnares them, and deceives them, and always intends herself for her end.

"But grace walks with simplicity, declines from all appearance of evil, offers no deceits, and does all things purely for God, in Whom also she rests as in her last end."   S. THOMAS A KEMPIS.

THE life in Christ, towards which our meditations till Easter must now tend, is a simple life.

In it there is no conscious effort after effect, no thought of appearances, no listening to opposing words, nor heeding distracting thoughts, no setting up of ourselves, no judging of others.

A simple life is a true life, a straight and sincere life without affectation, without doubts or fears, but able by the light of its own truthfulness to see and to love the truth of God.

The life of simplicity is a life of leaning upon God, a life of dependence on the promises of Christ, and of unfaltering confidence in God. As children cling to their parents, so does the simple child-like soul hold fast the Hand of God.

To the simple, God gives grace and wisdom far beyond any learning this world can bestow, therefore is a simple life one which rejoices in the Light of God. "If thine eye be single thy whole body shall be full of light," for God giveth grace to the simple.

The soul that is emptied of self shall be filled with all the fulness of God.

> "Come, ye little children,
> Unto Me draw nigh,
> For 'tis such as you
> That dwell with Me on high.

"Who, in truth and meekness,
   From all malice free,
   Ever serve and love Me
   With simplicity.

I, Who pride and greatness
   Evermore abase,
   On the poor and lowly
   Lavish all my grace;
   And to humble spirits
   Heavenly things reveal,
   Which my secret judgments
   From the proud conceal."

Aspiration.
"*Thy kingdom come.*"

Voice of Jesus.
"SUFFER THE LITTLE CHILDREN, AND FORBID THEM NOT TO COME UNTO ME, FOR OF SUCH IS THE KINGDOM OF HEAVEN."

Read *Psalm viii.* Lesson, *2 Cor. i. 2 to 13.*

Litany of the Holy Ghost.

Fourth Tuesday in Lent.

RECEPTIVITY.

"I LOOK FOR THE LORD, MY SOUL DOTH WAIT FOR HIM."—PSALM CXXX. 5.

"HE CAME UNTO HIS OWN, AND HIS OWN RECEIVED HIM NOT, BUT AS MANY AS RECEIVED HIM TO THEM GAVE HE POWER TO BECOME THE SONS OF GOD."—S. JOHN I. 11, 12.

Fourth Tuesday in Lent.

> "*Thou oughtest to seek the grace of devotion earnestly, to ask it fervently, to wait for it patiently and confidently, to receive it thankfully, to keep it humbly, to work with it diligently, and to commit to God the time and manner of this heavenly visitation, until it shall please Him to come unto Thee.*
>
> "*God often giveth in one short moment what He hath a long time denied.*
>
> "*Therefore, the grace of devotion is to be expected with a good hope and humble patience.*
>
> "*Whosoever with a single heart shall direct his intention upwards to God, and purify himself from all inordinate love or dislike of any created thing, he shall be the most fit to receive grace, and worthy of the gift of devotion.*"
>
> S. THOMAS A KEMPIS.

GOD is ready, "waiting to be gracious" unto us. He calls to us to open our mouths, that He may fill them.

Our position should be that of the little birds in their nest, quietly waiting in undoubting patience to be fed from our Father's Hand.

This is the attitude most pleasing to Him, because it shows entire dependence on God, and want of reliance on self.

It is not by the constant rushing hither and thither, and hurrying to and fro, it is not by greetings in the market place, and loud talking on platforms, it is not even by a perpetual round of schools, and visiting, or even religious services, that the heart is made ready to receive its Lord.

His great Forerunner, who was elected to prepare the way of Christ, dwelt from his childhood in the wilderness, and even when the necessities of his ministry called him into public notice, his great desire was to hide himself in the shadow of Him Whose shoe's latchet he said he "was not worthy to unloose."

So with the Blessed Mother of Jesus. She from whom

He vouchsafed to take His Human Nature, she who was privileged to bear the Incarnate Son of God, and to nourish and support His tender infancy, is yet as it were hidden in the cloud of glory which encircles her Divine Son. How quiet, how still was her humble life on earth, how slight the record of her on whom the benediction of all generations rests.

In the Life, too, of our dear Master Himself, there is the same stillness and quiet waiting upon God. For thirty years He Who was the glory of the Father, and "the express Image of His Person," lived a hidden secret life in the quiet home at Nazareth. For three years only was He seen and known of men, and much even of that short time He spent in lonely seclusion, on the mountain-top or in a desert place, absorbed in prayer to God, and the great consummation of His wondrous Life, was an act of passive endurance, when He suffered others to bind Him and carry Him to the death, from which His Human Heart must needs shrink with pain.

The greatest victory the world has ever seen, the glorious triumph which Saints and Angels celebrate, without ceasing before the Throne of God, was achieved by One Who was nailed fast to the cruel Tree, and unable to remove for one moment even His most sacred Hands and Feet.

Let us then learn from His sacred wounds to look for the Lord, and to wait patiently for Him, much in silence, much in prayer, while the sigh goes up from our hearts, "Come, Lord Jesus; come Holy Ghost, the comforter, and abide with us."

"Those voices low and gentle,
 And timid glances shy,
 That seem for aid parental
  To sue all wistfully.
Still pressing, longing to be right,
 Yet fearing to be wrong,
In these the pastor dares delight,
 A lamb-like, Christ-like throng.

These in life's distant even
 Shall shine serenely bright,
As in th' autumnal heaven
 Mild rainbow tints at night.
When the last shower is stealing down,
 And ere they sink to rest,
The sunbeams weave a parting crown
 For some sweet woodland nest."

Aspiration.
"*Master, we have toiled all night, and have taken nothing.*"

Voice of Jesus.
"IF ANY MAN THIRST, LET HIM COME TO ME AND DRINK."

Read *Psalm xlii.* Lesson, *Isa. lv.*

Litany of the Holy Ghost.

Fifth Wednesday in Lent.

DISCIPLESHIP.

"BEHOLD, O LORD, THAT I AM THY SERVANT."
"THE DISCIPLE IS NOT ABOVE HIS MASTER, BUT EVERY ONE THAT IS PERFECT SHALL BE AS HIS MASTER."—S. LUKE VI. 40.

"Lord, all things are Thine that are in Heaven and earth.

"I desire to offer up myself to Thee as a voluntary oblation, and to remain for ever Thine.

"Lord, in the sincerity of my heart I offer myself to Thee this day to be Thy servant evermore, to serve Thee, and to become a sacrifice of perpetual praise to Thee.

"Forgive, O my God, forgive me my sins for Thy Holy Name's sake. Save my soul which Thou hast redeemed with Thy Precious Blood.

"Behold, I commit myself to Thy mercy; I resign myself into Thy Hands.

"I offer to Thee all the good I have, though very little and imperfect; that Thou mayest make it better, and sanctify it; that Thou mayest be pleased with it, and make it acceptable to Thee, and perfect it more and more, and mayest moreover bring me, who am a slothful and unprofitable wretch, to a good and happy end.

"If thou desire to be My disciple, offer up thyself to Me with all thy affections." S. THOMAS A KEMPIS.

THE dear Master says. "Learn of Me." Let us, then, meditate to-day on our discipleship to Him, which means our way of learning what He teaches.

"The oil, which in the early days of the Church was used in Confirmation, consisted of two ingredients, balm and olive oil; the balm, which ever sinks below all other liquors, represents humility, and the oil of olives, which swims always above, represents meekness which surmounts all things, and excels amongst virtues as being the flower of charity, which S. Bernard says reaches its perfection when it is not only patient but also meek and mild."

Humility and meekness, then, must be the leading features in the disciples of Him Who said, "Learn of Me, for I am meek and lowly of heart."

Another characteristic of true discipleship is the imitation

Fifth Wednesday in Lent.

of the master by his followers. See how like to our Blessed Lord His Apostles and dearest friends became; how S. Peter, even in the manner of his death, was "as his Master;" how S. John spoke in the same words the Lord had used so long before, "Little children love one another;" how S. Stephen, who had seen Jesus only in a vision, yet died like his Master with a prayer for his enemies on his lips.

True discipleship, faithful learning of Jesus, must mould us to be like Him. It must teach us to love what He loved, and to despise only what He condemned.

His Blessed Presence has sanctified the earth on which we live, so that we must call nothing which He has touched either "common or unclean." His Presence has sancified the state of poverty, therefore are the poor of this world rich in the Sight of God. He has sanctified a life of self-denial and mortification, so must His disciples take up their cross and follow Him away from the luxuries and pleasures of the world; He has sanctified a death of pain and shame, shall we not count it joy to suffer with our Lord?

> "Dread crown of thorns which Jesus wore,
> Pledge of His dying Love,
> When clouds arise and tempests roar
> Shine on me from above.
>
> O let the points that pierced Thy Brow,
> Transpierce this faithless breast,
> That thought, and will, and wish, and vow,
> In Christ may ever rest."

Aspiration.
"My Lord and my God."

Voice of Jesus.
"WHOSOEVER DOTH NOT BEAR HIS CROSS AND COME AFTER ME, CANNOT BE MY DISCIPLE."

Read *Psalm cxviii.* Lesson, *S. Luke xiv. 25 to 34.*

Litany of our Lord Jesus Christ.

Fifth Thursday in Lent.

FRIENDSHIP WITH JESUS.

"WE TOOK SWEET COUNSEL TOGETHER, AND WALKED IN THE HOUSE OF GOD AS FRIENDS."—PSALM LV. 15.

"HENCEFORTH I CALL YOU NOT SERVANTS: FOR THE SERVANT KNOWETH NOT WHAT HIS LORD DOETH; BUT I HAVE CALLED YOU FRIENDS, FOR ALL THINGS THAT I HAVE HEARD OF MY FATHER I HAVE MADE KNOWN UNTO YOU."—S. JOHN XV. 15.

"*Who will give me, O Lord, to find Thee alone, that I may open my whole heart to Thee, and enjoy Thee as my soul desireth: no one beholding me, nor any creature interesting me, or at all affecting me; but Thou alone speaking to me, and I to Thee, as the Beloved is wont to speak to His Beloved, and a friend to entertain himself with his friend.*

"*This I pray for, this I desire, that I may be wholly united to Thee, and may withdraw my heart from all created things.*

"*Ah, Lord God! when shall I be wholly united to Thee, and absorbed in Thee, and altogether forgetful of myself.*

"*Thou in me, and I in Thee: and so grant us both to continue in one.*

"*Verily, Thou art my Beloved, the choicest among thousands, in Whom my soul is well pleased to dwell all the days of her life.*"

S. THOMAS A KEMPIS.

Fifth Thursday in Lent.

As we approach the great mysteries of the Passion and Resurrection of our Lord, our meditations must bring us ever nearer and more near to Him.

Yesterday we thought of discipleship, to-day we consider the far closer tie of friendship with the dear Master.

The disciple opens the door of his heart, that he may hear his Master's Voice, and learn of Him, the friend goes out to meet Him, and presses Him to come in and abide in his house; the disciple follows his Master even to prison and death, but the friend walks side by side with Him, and holds His Hand. Andrew and Philip and Thomas went with our Lord in His journeyings, and sat with Him at supper, but S. John leant upon His Breast.

Friendship is the going out of one heart to meet another, it is the touching and close union of the innermost part of man with man. Passion is selfish, and therefore passionate love seeks its own gratification in the object of its affection, but friendship seeks not her own, but goes out of self to unite her thoughts, and affections, and aspirations, with those of another, and a kindred, soul.

Let us think, then, if earthly friendship be so precious and so holy a thing, what must be the blessedness of him who is a friend of Jesus, who, like S. John, is a disciple whom Jesus loves, and to whom He will reveal the Will of His Father, Who is in Heaven?

Three things are necessary to those who would be friends of Jesus. They must leave all else for Him, they must be of the same mind with Him, they must do the work which He calls them to do.

Abraham, amongst the Old Testament Saints, was called the "Friend of God." Why? Because he left home and friends and country, and went out into a strange land, not knowing whither he went, but holding fast to the God Who led him by his hand. And it pleased God to make of him a nation, more than the stars of Heaven for multitude.

So is it ever with the friends of God. He makes them that they shall not be barren nor unfruitful, but after their death their works follow them, and their children call them blessed.

"Love abhors generalities." It is not content to say "Thou art the Lord," but the utterance of the loving heart is rather, "My Beloved is mine, and I am His;" "My Lord and my God."

> "Jesu, what didst Thou find in me,
> That Thou hast dealt so lovingly?
> How great the joy that Thou hast brought,
> So far exceeding hope or thought.
>
> Jesu, of Thee shall be my song,
> To Thee my heart and soul belong;
> All that I have or am is Thine,
> And Thou, sweet Saviour, Thou art mine.
> Jesu, my Lord, I Thee adore,
> O make me love Thee more and more."

Aspiration.
"*Lord, Thou knowest that I love Thee.*"

Voice of Jesus.
"IF I, YOUR LORD AND MASTER, HAVE WASHED YOUR FEET, YE ALSO OUGHT TO WASH ONE ANOTHER'S FEET."

Read *Psalm* lv. Lesson, *S. James* iv. *1-11.*

Litany of our Lord Jesus Christ.

Fifth Friday in Lent.

FELLOWSHIP IN SUFFERING.

"IN THE MULTITUDE OF THE SORROWS THAT I HAD IN MY HEART, THY COMFORTS HAVE REFRESHED MY SOUL."—PSALM XCIV. 19.

"THAT I MAY KNOW HIM, AND THE POWER OF HIS RESURRECTION, AND THE FELLOWSHIP OF HIS SUFFERINGS, BEING MADE CONFORMABLE UNTO HIS DEATH."—PHIL. III. 10.

"*Lord Jesus, I have received the cross, I have received it from Thy Hand, and I will bear it until death, as Thou hast laid it upon me. Indeed, the life of a good religious man is a cross, but it is a cross that conducts him to Paradise.*

"*Take courage, my brethren, let us go forward together; Jesus will be with us.*

"*For the sake of Jesus we took up His cross; for the sake of Jesus let us persevere in it.*

"*He will be our helper, Who is our captain and our leader.*

"*Let us follow Him like men of courage; let no one shrink through fear; let us be ready valiantly to die in battle, and not suffer our glory to be tarnished by flying from the Standard of the Cross.*"

S. THOMAS A KEMPIS.

THE return of Friday once more calls us to the thought of suffering, and we see that the closest tie of friendship with our Blessed Lord is to " know the fellowship of His sufferings."

Nothing draws earthly friends together more nearly than suffering which they bear together, in and for each other. Even those who have been our enemies are sometimes drawn to us and made into friends by the softening touch of suffering and pain.

In a far higher degree does the fellowship of the sufferings of our Divine Master knit our hearts to His Loving Heart, and hold us close to Him.

This holy fellowship teaches us what a blessed thing it is to suffer like the Lord. The cross, since He deigned to hang on it, shines with the glory of His Presence, and lights up the darkest day; the crown of thorns, since it touched His Sacred Brow, has become a diadem of precious jewels which the Saints delight to wear; the nails, since His Blessed Hands and Feet were pierced with them, are now to His faithful children, but a welcome means by which they are more firmly united to the Passion of their Lord.

To know the fellowship of His sufferings is to find comfort in affliction, joy in grief, and peace in that death by which we are made conformable to Him.

So did the Saints win their crown of glory, and triumph over the bitterest of torments, because in the midst of their cruellest sufferings they rejoiced in the sight of Him Who is invisible, Who bore all their griefs and carried all their sorrows.

> "Pierce through my feet, my hands, my heart,
>   It may some drop distil
> Of Blood Divine into my soul,
>   And all its evils heal.
>
> So shall my feet be slow to sin,
>   Harmless my hands shall be;
> So from my wounded heart shall each
>   Forbidden passion flee."

Fifth Saturday in Lent.

Aspiration.
"*We receive the due reward of our deeds.*"

Voice of Jesus.
"HE THAT LOVETH HIS LIFE SHALL LOSE IT; AND HE THAT HATETH HIS LIFE IN THIS WORLD SHALL KEEP IT UNTO LIFE ETERNAL."

Read *Psalm xxiii.* Lesson, *1 S. Peter iv.*

Litany of the Passion.

Fifth Saturday in Lent.

READINESS.

"O GOD, MY HEART IS READY, MY HEART IS READY."—PSALM CVIII. 1.

"IF THERE BE FIRST A WILLING MIND, IT IS ACCEPTED ACCORDING TO THAT A MAN HATH, AND NOT ACCORDING TO THAT HE HATH NOT."—2 COR. VIII. 12.

"*As I willingly offered Myself to God My Father, for thy sins, with My Hands stretched out on the Cross, even so must thou willingly offer thyself to Me daily for a pure and holy oblation, together with all thy powers and affections, as heartily as thou art able.*

"*Whatever thou givest besides thyself, I regard not; for I seek not thy gift, but thyself.*

"*Therefore, before all thy works, thou must make a free oblation of thyself into the Hands of God, if thou desire to obtain liberty and grace.*

"*If thou desire to be My disciple, offer up thyself to Me, with all thy affections.*"   S. THOMAS A KEMPIS.

LET us meditate to-day on the readiness of mind wherewith we should be waiting to receive all the blessings of a close and intimate communion with our dear Lord and Master.

He has called us; He is always calling us to follow Him; every day this Lent His Voice has sounded in our ears; how have we responded to the call?

Have we said with S. Paul, "Lord, I am ready to be offered?" or have we begun at once to make excuses? Have the farm, or the merchandize, or the wife, filled our minds, and left no place for the Lord, Who gave them all, and meant us to use them all to draw us nearer to Himself?

Nothing must come before Jesus and His Word. If He says "come," we must go with Him, nor must any obligations to friends, or relations, or home, or work, hold us for a moment back from Him. Not even to bury an earthly father must we delay to obey the summons of our Father in Heaven.

God is very merciful, and He asks but few sacrifices at our hands. The duties He imposes on us are for the most part so bound up with our affections and interests, that the more truly we serve Him, the more faithful are we to those with whom He has placed us.

But He requires of us a willing mind, ready at any moment to give up to Him everything that we have, everything that we love, if He requires us to do so.

He may try our faith and love, even to demand of us the offering of the one precious child of our old age, the one in whom, as in Isaac, all our hopes and promises are bound up, and we must bind the sacrifice with cords, and be ready to give up our only son to Him.

Has He not given His only Son for us? and if, at the

Fifth Saturday in Lent.

last moment, when He sees that we are wholly conformed to His Will, He should stay the sacrificial Hand, and accept a lesser gift instead, it is only one more proof of His Mercy and His Love, Who will so frame the trial that we may be able to bear it.

"Let Him do what seemeth Him good," was the utterance of a Patriarch.

"Be it unto me according to Thy Word," was the utterance of the greatest of all the Saints, on whom shall rest the benediction of all generations of the children of God.

"My meat is to do the Will of Him that sent Me," is the utterance of Him to Whom we ever look for guidance, the Alpha and Omega of our faith and Love.

"Grant us pure wisdom to attain,
And fervent charity to gain;
Oh! surest Heaven-descended sign,
Of them that please Thy Will Divine.

Now Thy sweet promise we believe,
How they that ask shall more receive;
So may Thine own free mercy grant
All other gifts Thy servants want."

Aspiration.
"Lord, I am not worthy that Thou shouldest come under my roof."

Voice of Jesus.
"YE HAVE NOT CHOSEN ME, BUT I HAVE CHOSEN YOU, AND ORDAINED YOU, THAT YE SHOULD GO AND BRING FORTH FRUIT, AND THAT YOUR FRUIT SHOULD REMAIN."

Read *Psalm cviii. 1.* Lesson, *1 S. Peter ii. 1-11.*

Litany of the Holy Ghost.

Fifth Sunday in Lent.

THE LAW OF SACRIFICE.

"OPEN THOU MINE EYES, THAT I MAY SEE THE WONDROUS THINGS OF THY LAW."—PSALM CIX. 18.

"WITHOUT SHEDDING OF BLOOD IS NO REMISSION."—HEB. IX. 22.

" Moses, Thy servant, Thy great and special friend, made an ark of incorruptible wood, which he also covered with most pure gold, that he might deposit therein the tables of the Law. Solomon, the wisest of the kings of Israel, employed seven years in building a magnificent temple for the praise of Thy Name; and for eight days together celebrated the feast of the dedication thereof. He offered a thousand pacific victims, and brought the Ark of the Covenant in a solemn manner into the place prepared for it.

" Oh! my God, how much did they endeavour to do to please Thee? Alas! how little it is that I do.

"And yet there is a great difference between those sacrifices of the law, which were figures of things to come, and the true sacrifice of Thy Body, which is the accomplishing of all those ancient sacrifices. Why do I not prepare myself with greater care to receive Thy sacred gifts, seeing that these ancient holy Patriarchs and Prophets, yea, kings also, and princes, with the whole people, have shewed so great affection of devotion towards Thy Divine Worship?"   S. THOMAS A KEMPIS.

THE Epistle appointed for this fifth Sunday in Lent brings our Blessed Lord before us as the High Priest of good things to come, entering into the Holy Place, not with the blood of bulls and of goats, as required by the old covenant, but by His own Blood, "having obtained eternal redemption for us."

Let us meditate to-day on the great Law of Sacrifice, which

Fifth Sunday in Lent.

is the very foundation of all the ordinances and dispensations of Almighty God.

Since Adam fell, it has been the great and unchanging Law of God that sin could only be purged away by blood. Under the old dispensation the "blood of bulls and of goats" streamed from the altars where innocent victims gave their lives to make an atonement for the sins of the people.

Under the new dispensation of the glorious Gospel of Christ the Most Precious Blood of Him Who was Priest and Victim too, flowed on the Altar of the Cross for the eternal redemption of the whole world.

A great writer has said, "Sacrifice is the key of the difficulties of the dogmas of the Church, it is the soul of its mysteries, the cause of its asceticism, the pattern of its mystical union with God.

"Ritual is the action of sacrifice; prayer is the language of sacrifice; contemplation is the thought of sacrifice; and interior mortification is sacrifice itself."

May God help us during this sacred week, so to meditate on this great Law of Sacrifice that we may be prepared in body and soul to kneel beneath the Saviour's Cross on Good Friday, and to welcome Him with pure hearts full of love and praise, when He shall give Himself to us in Communion at Eastertide.

> "Both theirs and ours Thou art,
> As we and they are Thine,
> Kings, Prophets, Patriarchs, all have part
> Along the sacred line.

> " By blood and water, too,
>   God's mark is set on Thee,
>   That in Thee every faithful view
>   Both covenants might see."

Aspiration.
" *Master, what shall I do to inherit Eternal Life?*"

Voice of Jesus.
"WHAT IS WRITTEN IN THE LAW; HOW READEST THOU?"

Read *Psalm l.* Lesson, *Hebrews x. 1-14.*

Litany of Penitence.

Fifth Monday in Lent.

SACRIFICE OF LOVE.

"BECAUSE HE HATH SET HIS LOVE UPON ME, THEREFORE WILL I DELIVER HIM, I WILL SET HIM UP BECAUSE HE HATH KNOWN MY NAME."—PSALM XCI. 14.

"SET ME AS A SEAL UPON THINE HEART, AS A SEAL UPON THINE ARM; FOR LOVE IS STRONG AS DEATH."—SONG OF SOLOMON VIII. 6.

"*Verily Thou art my Beloved, the choicest among thousands, in whom my soul is well pleased to dwell all the days of her life.*

" *Thou art in truth a hidden God, and Thy counsel is not with the wicked; but Thy conversation is with the humble and the simple.*

" *Surely there is no other nation so great that hath their God so nigh to them as Thou our God art present to Thy faithful. For what other nation is there so honoured as the Christian people?*

" *Or what creature under Heaven so beloved as a devout soul, into whom God cometh?*

"*O infinite love, singularly bestowed upon man.*

"*But what return shall I make to the Lord for this grace?*

Fifth Monday in Lent.

"There is nothing that I can give Him that will please Him better than if I give up my heart entirely to God, and unite it closely to Him."

S. THOMAS A KEMPIS.

GOD will not accept at our hands anything less than the best we have to offer.

He estimates the value of the sacrifice, not by its own intrinsic worth, but by the proportion it bears to the value of His gifts to us.

It is "of His own" that we give Him, be it much or little, for we have nothing that we did not first receive from Him.

The offering of the mite which the widow put into the treasury of God, and the offering of the costly alabaster box of precious ointment which was broken and poured out in the service of the Divine Master—these two gifts met with the same gracious reception and approval from our Blessed Lord, because in each case the giver had done all she could.

The best gift we have to offer, is the sacrifice of the affections of our hearts, and this is the only sacrifice that is acceptable in the Sight of God, because the affections are the highest, and best, and most God-like part of our weak human nature.

If we do not offer the fervent love of our hearts, the first and highest place in our affections, to the God Who made us and keeps us in being, He will not accept anything that we may try to offer Him instead.

The first and great commandment is this, "Thou shalt love the Lord thy God."

True, we cannot see Him, though He is our Father, but we are to look for Him in His works and in His Word, and more than all, we are to learn to know and to love Him in His Son, our most Blessed and only Lord; and as, by the help of the Holy Spirit we learn more of Him, we cannot fail to give Him the first place in our hearts, for who can satisfy the soul as He does? Where is there any happiness like that of knowing Christ, and being found in Him?

"Then all that is within me shall rejoice exceedingly when my soul shall be perfectly united to my God: then will He say to me: If thou wilt be with Me, I will be with thee: and I will answer Him, Vouchsafe, O Lord, to remain with me, and I will willingly be with Thee."

Lord, I desire to bring a loving heart to the Altar of Thy Cross.

"Jesus, would our hearts were burning
With more burning love for Thee,
Would our eyes were ever turning
To Thy Cross of Agony.

So in pain and rapture blending
Might our failing eyes grow dim,
While the freed heart rose, ascending
To the circling cherubim.

Then in glory, parted never
From the Saviour's sheltering side,
Graven on our hearts for ever
Be the Cross and Crucified."

Aspiration.

"*Let us not love in word, but in deed and in truth.*"

Voice of Jesus.

"GREATER LOVE HATH NO MAN THAN THIS, THAT A MAN LAY DOWN HIS LIFE FOR HIS FRIENDS."

Read *Psalm cxlv.* Lesson, *1 S. John ii. 1-8.*

Litany of the Passion.

Fifth Tuesday in Lent.

SACRIFICE OF THANKSGIVING.

"WHOSO OFFERETH ME THANKS AND PRAISE HE HONOURETH ME," PSALM L. 23.

" BE FILLED WITH THE SPIRIT."

"GIVING THANKS ALWAYS FOR ALL THINGS UNTO GOD AND THE FATHER, IN THE NAME OF OUR LORD JESUS CHRIST."—EPH. V. 18, 20.

" *O Father of mercies and God of all comfort, I give thanks to Thee, Who art pleased to cherish with Thy consolation, me that am unworthy of any comfort.*

"*I bless and glorify Thee for evermore, together with Thy only-begotten Son and the Holy Ghost, the Comforter, to all eternity.*

"*Let me love Thee more than myself, and myself only for Thee, and all others in Thee, who truly love Thee as the law of love commands, which shines forth from Thee.*

"*Love is submissive and obedient; in its own eyes mean and contemptible; devout and thankful to God, always trusting and hoping in Him, even then, when it tastes not the relish of God's sweetness; for there is no living in love without some pain and sorrow.*"   THOMAS A KEMPIS.

A LOVING heart must be a thankful heart, for is it not the thought of all His mercies towards us, which kindles in our hearts true love to God, and makes us long to offer to Him continually a sacrifice of praise and thanksgiving?

No better exercise can there be for the soul than to count up, and tell over and over again, all the mercies God has bestowed on her. The more we think of them, the more their number grows, for as we meditate, we see that even troubles and trials were mercies in disguise, mercies for which we must give thanks to the Giver of all good.

Let us, then, thank God continually, and offer our daily sacrifice of loving, grateful hearts.

Let us thank Him for our life and breath, for our daily bread, for all the loving ties with which He has bound us to each other, for His Holy Church and His Word, for all the sorrows whereby He trains our souls for Heaven, for the Communion of Saints, for the blessed grace of the Sacraments, above and beyond all, for the Precious Gifts of His dear Son, by Whose Life our life is sanctified, and by Whose Death our souls are saved from death, and are admitted into the Presence of the Lord.

Let us not go on our way towards the deep mysteries of the Holy Week, without first returning along the road we have come, that "we may kneel at the Feet of Jesus, and give glory to God" for our deliverance from the leprosy of sin.

> "When all Thy mercies, O my God,
>   My rising soul surveys,
> Transported with the view, I'm lost
>   In wonder, love, and praise.
>
> Ten thousand, thousand, precious gifts,
>   My daily thanks employ;
> Nor is the least a thankful heart
>   That tastes those gifts with joy.
>
> Through all eternity, to Thee
>   A joyful song I'll raise;
> But oh! eternity's too short
>   To utter all Thy praise."

Aspiration.
"*Hallowed be Thy Name.*"

Voice of Jesus.
"I THANK THEE, O FATHER, LORD OF HEAVEN AND EARTH, THAT THOU HAST HID THESE THINGS FROM THE WISE AND PRUDENT, AND HAST REVEALED THEM UNTO BABES."

Read *Psalm xcii.* Lesson, *S. Luke xvii. 11-20.*

Litany of the Holy Ghost.

Sixth Wednesday in Lent.

SACRIFICE OF OBEDIENCE.

"PAY THY VOWS UNTO THE MOST HIGHEST."—PSALM L. 14.

"IN BURNT OFFERINGS AND SACRIFICES FOR SIN THOU HAST HAD NO PLEASURE. THEN SAID I, LO I COME (IN THE VOLUME OF THE BOOK IT IS WRITTEN OF ME) TO DO THY WILL, O GOD."—HEB. X. 6, 7.

"*Lord, all things are Thine that are in Heaven and earth.*

"*I desire to offer up myself to Thee as a voluntary oblation, and to remain for ever Thine.*

"*Lord, in the sincerity of my heart I offer myself to Thee this day to be Thy servant evermore, to serve Thee, and to become a sacrifice of perpetual praise to Thee.*

"*Receive me with the Sacred Oblation of Thy Precious Body in the presence of Thy angels standing invisibly by.*

"*Behold, I commit myself to Thy mercy; I resign myself into Thy Hands.*

"*I offer to Thee all the good I have, though very little and imperfect; that Thou mayest make it better, and sanctify it; that Thou mayest be pleased with it, and make it acceptable to Thee, and perfect it more and more; and mayest bring me to a good and happy end.*"

THOMAS A KEMPIS.

OBEDIENCE is the test of the reality of the other sacrifices which we offer to God.

The reality of the love and thanksgiving which we offer must be proved by our readiness to do "whatsoever He commands us."

"Whatsoever" is an all-embracing word. The sacrifice of obedience knows no mitigation, allows of no reserve. As the Passover lamb was to be roasted whole and complete, so must every part of us be laid on the Altar of God, and offered up to Him.

He will accept no less. To keep anything back is to make the offering vain and worthless in the sight of God. Body, soul, and spirit, He created us, to love and serve Him, and body, soul, and spirit, we must offer in their entirety to Him.

This perfection of obedience can be learned only beneath the Cross, as we meditate on the Incarnation of the Eternal Son of God.

The Incarnation was the consummation of obedience, the absolute fulfilment of the Almighty Will of God.

Therefore must we, in order that our sacrifice may be accepted on high, unite it to the sacrifice of the Incarnate Son of God.

The more we meditate on the life and death of the Lord, the more we exercise our souls in the study of each most sweet and holy mystery of the Incarnation, the more we shall find that our wills, and desires, and aspirations, grow into conformity with Him.

In Him alone can our "whole body and soul and spirit

be preserved blameless" unto His coming again. By Him, and through the Great Mystery of His Incarnation alone, can we offer up ourselves to God in that perfect obedience which is our "reasonable service."

> "'Tis Thy good pleasure, not my own,
> In Thee, my God, I love alone;
> And nothing I desire of Thee
> But what Thy goodness wills for me.
>
> To Thee I consecrate and give
> My heart and being while I live;
> Jesus, Thy Heart alone shall be
> My love for all eternity.
> May Heaven and earth with love fulfil,
> My God, Thy ever-blessed Will."

Aspiration.
"*Thy Will be done on earth, as it is in Heaven.*"

Voice of Jesus.
"IF A MAN LOVE ME, HE WILL KEEP MY WORDS."

Read *Psalm l.* Lesson, *Hebrews v*

Litany of our Lord Jesus Christ.

Sixth Thursday in Lent.

SACRIFICE OF PRAISE.

"O SING PRAISES, SING PRAISES UNTO OUR GOD; O SING PRAISES, SING PRAISES UNTO OUR KING."—PSALM XLVII. 6.

"BY HIM, THEREFORE, LET US OFFER THE SACRIFICE OF PRAISE TO GOD CONTINUALLY, THAT IS, THE FRUIT OF OUR LIPS."—HEB. VIII. 15.

> "*O Lord my God, my Creator, and my Redeemer, I desire to receive Thee with such affection, reverence, praise, and honour as Thy Holy Mother received and desired Thee.*
>
> "*Wherefore, I here offer and present to Thee the excessive joys of all devout hearts, their ardent affections and ecstacies, together with all the virtues and praises which are, or shall be, celebrated by all creatures in Heaven and earth; for myself and all such as are recommended to my prayers; that by all Thou mayest be worthily praised and glorified for ever.*
>
> "*Let all peoples, tribes, and tongues praise Thee, and magnify Thy Holy and sweet Name, with the highest jubilation and ardent devotion.*"
>
> THOMAS A KEMPIS.

As the Sacrifice of the Cross gives a solemn sacredness to every Friday in the year, so does the glory of the Holy Eucharist, our great Sacrifice of Praise, light up with its radiance every Thursday in every week, and especially this Thursday, which is the forerunner of the great Thursday which is exalted for ever in a Christian's eyes by the Institution of the most Blessed Sacrament of the Body and Blood of Christ.

Next Thursday we shall hope with due awe and reverence to commemorate that holy Institution, and it is well for us now to tune our hearts to the sweet melody of praise with which the voice of the Church shall celebrate her Eucharistic Feast.

Love and thanksgiving are the mind and soul of sacrifice, obedience is the action of sacrifice, and praise is the expression of sacrifice; the sweet melody which underlies and accompanies all the varying harmonies of the Gospel of the Incarnation of the Word of God.

Out of the abundance of a loving, grateful heart the song of praise will burst forth, even the fruit of our lips rejoicing in the beauty of the Lord.

Sixth Thursday in Lent.

Only let us remember that it is only a pure heart which makes melody to the Lord. Corrupt and sordid thoughts destroy all the beauty of the song, and make it jangle out of tune: there must be no discords in the anthem which we raise to God. It must be the echo of the angels' song before the throne, a pure and lofty hymn of praise to the honour and glory of our God, and such a sacrifice is well pleasing in His Sight.

"Praise ye the Lord; on every height
Songs to His glory raise.
Ye angel hosts, ye stars of night,
Send forth your voice of praise,
For His the word that gave you birth,
And majesty, and might;
Praise to the Highest from the earth,
And let the depths unite.

Ye judges, rulers, kings, whose hand
The sceptre waves on high;
O youths and virgins of the land,
O age and infancy;
Praise ye His Name, to Him alone
All homage should be given,
Whose glory from th' Eternal Throne
Spreads wide o'er earth and Heaven."

Aspiration.

"*Blessed is He that cometh in the Name of the Lord, Hosanna in the Highest.*"

Voice of Jesus.

"HEREAFTER SHALL YE SEE THE SON OF MAN SITTING ON THE RIGHT HAND OF POWER, AND COMING IN THE CLOUDS OF HEAVEN."

Read *Psalm viii.* Lesson, *Eph. v. 13 to 22.*

Litany of our Lord Jesus Christ.

Sixth Friday in Lent.

JOY OF SACRIFICE.

"THEN SHALT THOU BE PLEASED WITH THE SACRIFICE OF RIGHTEOUSNESS, WITH THE BURNT OFFERINGS AND OBLATIONS: THEN SHALL THEY OFFER YOUNG BULLOCKS UPON THINE ALTAR."—PSALM LI. 19.

"YE SHALL BE SORROWFUL, BUT YOUR SORROW SHALL BE TURNED INTO JOY."—S. JOHN XVI. 20.

"*To glory in tribulation is not hard to him that loves; for so to glory is to glory in the Cross of our Lord.*

"*The joy of the just is from God and in God, and they rejoice in the Truth.*

"*Prepare thyself to bear tribulations, and account them the greatest consolations; for the sufferings of this life bear no proportion with the glory to come.*

"*When thou shalt arrive thus far, that tribulation becomes sweet and savoury to thee, for the love of Christ, then think that it is well with thee, for thou hast found a paradise upon earth.*

"*Would to God thou wert worthy to suffer something for the Name of Jesus! How great a glory would be laid up for thee, how great joy would it be to all the Saints of God.*" THOMAS A KEMPIS.

OUR Friday meditations have now brought us to the highest point which suffering can reach, even to that point at which it touches the Heart of Jesus, and is turned into joy, the joy of Angels, the joy of the Redeemed, the joy of all the hosts of Heaven, who rejoice with unceasing praise in "the Lamb as it had been slain."

No higher point can human suffering attain to than this, and it is a fit preparation for our consideration of that which is beyond and above all human attainment, the sufferings of God Incarnate in the flesh.

Next Friday we must lie prostrate before this most inscrutable and tremendous mystery of a suffering God.

To-day, we will try to realize somewhat of the nature of that joy which is the wondrous fruit of the tree of human sorrow, grief, and pain, nourished by the sap of the grace of God, and ripened by the light and warmth of the "Sun of Righteousness."

A great writer has said, "there is nothing on earth that is half so sweet as to think about God."

In these few words lies the secret of that wondrous joy "of suffering born." It is because pain, and suffering, and grief, and trouble of all sorts, if only we nail them to the Cross of Jesus, lift us nearer to God, and fill our hearts more entirely with thoughts of Him than any other condition of our life on earth.

The greater the sacrifice, the nearer will it bring us to God, the nearer we draw to God, the more our hearts are satisfied and filled with sweetness and with joy.

> "Jesu, the very thought of Thee
>   With sweetness fills the breast,
> But sweeter far Thy Face to see,
>   And in Thy Presence rest.
>
> O Hope of every contrite heart,
>   O Joy of all the meek,
> To those who fall how kind Thou art,
>   How good to those who seek.
>
> Jesu, our only Joy be Thou,
>   As Thou our Prize wilt be;
> Jesu, be Thou our glory now
>   And through eternity."

Aspiration.
"*I have sought Thee sorrowing.*"

Voice of Jesus.
"YOUR JOY NO MAN TAKETH FROM YOU."

Read *Psalm xcvii.* Lesson, *S. John xvi.* 12 to end.

Litany of the Passion.

Sixth Saturday in Lent.

CROWN OF SACRIFICE.

"THE RIGHTEOUS ALSO SHALL GIVE THANKS UNTO THY NAME, AND THE JUST SHALL CONTINUE IN THY SIGHT."—PSALM CXL. 13.

"THE GOD OF ALL GRACE, WHO HATH CALLED US UNTO HIS ETERNAL GLORY BY CHRIST JESUS, AFTER THAT YE HAVE SUFFERED A WHILE, MAKE YOU PERFECT, STABLISH, STRENGTHEN, SETTLE YOU."— I PET. V. 10.

"*They that perfectly despise the world, and study to live to God under holy discipline, experience the divine sweetness that is promised for those who forsake all: and such clearly see how grievously the world is mistaken, and how many ways it is deceived.*

"*Thou, Who art the Truth, hast plainly said, 'Where thy treasure is, there is also thy heart.'*

"*Blessed is the man, who for Thee, O Lord, lets go all the things created, who offers violence to his nature, and through fervour of spirit crucifies the lusts of the flesh; that so his conscience being cleared up, he may offer to Thee pure prayer, and may be worthy to be admitted among the choirs of angels, having shut out all things of the earth, both from without and within.*"

THOMAS A KEMPIS.

THE crown and glory of sacrifice can never be fully known in this world, for here we have no "continuing city," and whatever there is of good in us cannot here reach either its perfection, or its consummation and reward. The Lord Himself will give the crown when the good and faithful servant shall enter into His Presence on the further side of the valley of the shadow of death.

Yet it is profitable for us to meditate to-day on the crown and reward of sacrifice, because we need so much encouragement to help us on our way. The life of sacrifice is a difficult, and a hard one to live. The cross weighs heavily, the way is steep, and our feet are bruised and bleeding. Let us then thank God that He vouchsafes to open the clouds of Heaven, and in our darkest hour reveals to our sight a faint vision of the crown which the angels are holding for us, as they watch us on our way.

It is a beautiful crown, for it is one which the Lord Himself has prepared for us, and into it He has woven the golden cords of the love which drew us to follow Him, and round it He has placed bright jewels for every thorn whose prick we bore for Him, and in the fore-front of it He has placed His seal, which is to mark us as His own for ever, and to keep us safe from all sorrow and pain for ever, and for evermore.

Ah! so beautiful is the crown, that, as we think about it, it seems to make the life of sacrifice quite beautiful too, and we find so much consolation and joy in the way of the Cross, that we begin to fear lest, after all, we are only following our own will, and walking in our own way. So blessed a thing it is to lose ourselves in Jesus, and to offer ourselves, and all the desires of our hearts a willing sacrifice to Him.

> "The Cross that Jesus carried
> He carried as your due,
> The Crown that Jesus weareth
> He weareth it for you.
>
> The trials that beset you,
> The sorrows ye endure,
> The manifold temptations
> That death alone can cure
>
> What are they but His jewels,
> Of right celestial worth?
> What are they but the ladder
> Set up to Heaven on earth?"

Aspiration.
"Behold, we have forsaken all."

Voice of Jesus.
"EVERYONE THAT HATH FORSAKEN HOUSES, OR BRETHREN, OR SISTERS, OR FATHER, OR MOTHER, OR WIFE, OR CHILDREN, OR LANDS, FOR MY NAME'S SAKE, SHALL RECEIVE AN HUNDREDFOLD, AND SHALL INHERIT EVERLASTING LIFE."

Read *Psalm cxxxii.* Lessons, *Rev. ii. 1 to 11.*

Litany of our Lord Jesus Christ.

Sunday next before Easter.

REJOICING IN THE LORD.

"I WAS GLAD WHEN THEY SAID UNTO ME, WE WILL GO INTO THE HOUSE OF THE LORD."—PSALM CXXII. 1.

Sunday next before Easter.

"THE LORD WHOM YE SEEK SHALL SUDDENLY COME TO HIS TEMPLE, EVEN THE MESSENGER OF THE COVENANT WHOM YE DELIGHT IN."— MAL. III. 1.

"*O Jesus, the Brightness of eternal glory, the comfort of a soul in its pilgrimage; my tongue cannot express the sentiments of my heart; but my silence itself speaks to Thee.*

"*How long doth my Lord delay to come! Let Him come to me, His poor servant, and make me joyful; let Him stretch forth His Hand and deliver me.*

"*Come, for without Thee I can never have one joyful day nor hour, for Thou art my joy; and without Thee my table is empty.*

"*I am miserable, and in a manner imprisoned, till Thou comfort me with the light of Thy Presence, and restore me to liberty, and show me a favourable countenance.*

"*Let others seek, instead of Thee, whatever else they please; nothing else doth please me but Thou, my God, my hope, my eternal salvation.*"

THOMAS A KEMPIS.

Is it strange that this, the most solemn week of all the Christian year, should begin with a note of joy, the glad songs of children's voices, the shout of them that triumph and keep holy-day?

Yes, indeed, it is very meet, right, and our bounden duty "that we should on this day rejoice with the Lord, Who came on this day to visit His Temple, and rode through the palm-strewn streets of Jerusalem among the Hosannas of the multitude, meek and lowly, and sitting on a colt, the foal of an ass.

Let Judah be glad, and let the daughter of Zion rejoice, for behold! it is her King Who comes to her.

Let the Temple walls echo to the shout of praise, for the great High Priest is about to offer the one only perfect sacrifice by which atonement shall be made for sin for evermore.

So though we are entering on a week of profound mystery, the deep mystery of suffering, even of the suffering of God for man, yet may we to-day rejoice in the Lord, for God hath very highly exalted Him, and let us adore the Name which is above every name.

Yet though He be so high, He comes to us in meek and lowly guise, in the form of a servant, riding on an ass's colt. May the same mind be in us which was in Christ Jesus our Lord!

> "Lord, by every minstrel tongue
> Be Thy praise so duly sung,
> That Thine angels' harps may ne'er
> Fail to find fit echoing here.
> We the while, of meaner birth,
> Who in that divinest spell
> Dare not hope to join on earth,
> Give us grace to listen well."

Aspiration.
"*Thou, O Lord, art praised in Zion, and unto Thee shall the vow be performed in Jerusalem.*"

Voice of Jesus.
"I TELL YOU THAT IF THESE SHOULD HOLD THEIR PEACE, THE STONES WOULD IMMEDIATELY CRY OUT."

Read *Psalm xcvii.* Lesson, *S. Luke xix. 28 to 41.*

Litany of the Passion.

Monday before Easter.

THE MAN OF SORROWS.

"I AM POURED OUT LIKE WATER."—PSALM XXII. 14.
"BEHOLD, AND SEE IF THERE BE ANY SORROW LIKE UNTO MY SORROW?"—LAM. I. 12.

"*Son, I came down from Heaven for thy salvation; I took upon Me thy miseries, not of necessity, but moved thereto by charity, that thou mightest learn patience, and mightest bear without repining the miseries of this life.*

"*For from the hour of My birth, till My expiring on the Cross, I was never without suffering.*

"*I underwent a great want of temporal things: I frequently heard many complaints against Me: I meekly bore with confusion and reproaches: for My benefits I received ingratitude; for My miracles, blasphemies; and for My heavenly doctrine, reproaches.*

"*Cease then to complain, considering My Passion, and the sufferings of the Saints.*

"*Thou must call to mind the heavy sufferings of others, that thou mayest the easier bear the little things thou sufferest.*"
THOMAS A KEMPIS.

THE Services of the Church during this Holy Week bring before us so fully and so constantly all the solemn events of the Passion and Death of our Lord and Master, that I think it will be more profitable for us in our private meditations, to dwell more on what we may venture to call the lesser incidents of the Passion, which cluster round the great scene on Calvary as "the satellites round some great planet shine."

But first of all it behoves us to consider Him, by Whom,

and for Whom, all things consist, the "Great High Priest of our profession," in the mystery of Whose Incarnation we rest all our hopes for this world, and for that which is to come, by Whose sufferings and Death alone, we are sanctified and raised to the mansions of the blest.

Let us consider Him to-day by that Name so dear to every aching heart, the "Man of Sorrows," and may our thoughts dwell much with Him in Gethsemane, where in His agony His most precious Blood was shed.

There is not one pang that wrings His children's hearts but He has felt it first—weariness, hunger, exhaustion, the faithlessness of friends, the bitter malice of enemies, secret foes and outward opposition, disappointment—if one may say it—in those who seemed to have their hearts touched by His teaching. In addition to all these sorrows, He felt the pain which never afflicts the sons of men, by His Divine foresight of all the bitter agony and shame to which His daily Life was ever drawing more near, and then came the agonizing hour in Gethsemane, the betrayal, the cruel insults and scourging, the mocking, the crown of thorns, the nails, the spear. Was there ever any sorrow like unto His sorrow?

How beautiful He is, how gracious and how kind! Even in the utmost intensity of physical suffering, He prays for His murderers, and He binds up the broken heart of His Mother and His Friend!

He "has trodden the wine-press alone," that in our time of suffering we may never be alone, for He will come to help us. "In the greatness of His strength" shall He bear us up. He will lead us and comfort us, for He has made Himself a glorious Name. He is the "Man of Sorrows, and acquainted with grief."

"On thee and thine, thy warfare and thy end,
E'en in His hour of agony He thought,
When, ere the final pang His soul should rend,
The ransomed spirits one by one were brought
To His mind's eye—two silent nights and days
In calmness from His far-seen home He stays.

Miss we the light, Gethsemane, that streams
From thy dear name, where in His page of woe
It shines a pale, kind star in winter's sky,
Who vainly reads it there, in vain had seen Him die."

Aspiration.
"*Thou, O Lord, art our Father, our Redeemer, Thy Name is from everlasting.*"

Voice of Jesus.
"I, I AM HE THAT COMFORTETH."

Read *Psalm xxxiv.* Lesson, *S. Luke xxii. 39 to 47.*
Litany of the Passion.

Tuesday before Easter.

BETRAYED.

"IT WAS EVEN THOU, MY COMPANION: MY GUIDE, AND MINE OWN FAMILIAR FRIEND."—PSALM LV. 14.

"VERILY, VERILY, I SAY UNTO YOU, THAT ONE OF YOU SHALL BETRAY ME."—S. JOHN XIII. 21.

G

> "*In Thee, O Lord God, I put all my hope and refuge; to Thee I make known all my tribulation and anguish; for I find all to be infirm and unstable, whatever I behold out of Thee.*
>
> "*For neither will a multitude of friends be of any service to me; nor can strong auxiliaries bring me any succour, nor wise counsellors give me a profitable answer, nor the books of the learned comfort me, nor any wealth deliver me, nor any secret or pleasant place screen me, if Thou Thyself do not assist, help, strengthen, comfort, instruct, and defend me.*
>
> "*To Thee I lift up mine eyes; in Thee, O my God, the Father of mercies, I put my trust. Bless and sanctify my soul with Thy heavenly Blessing, that it may be made Thy holy habitation, and the seat of Thy eternal glory, and let nothing be found in the temple of Thy Dignity that may offend the eyes of Thy Majesty.*"
>
> THOMAS A KEMPIS.

No drop in all the cup of suffering which our dear Lord drank, could have been much more bitter to Him, than the woeful story of the traitor Judas.

Not only had Judas enjoyed a place among the twelve most intimate and close friends of Jesus, teaching with them, working with them, acting as treasurer to the little company, journeying about with the dear Master, and ever listening to His gracious Words; not only had he shared with the others all these blessed privileges, but he had been the object of a special effort on the part of his Lord to save him from the terrible sin which ruined him.

The Lord said so solemnly to them all, "Verily, verily, I say unto you, one of you shall betray Me," and when no one owned the temptation, though all were sorrowful at the saying, the Lord spoke yet more plainly, and pointed out His false follower even in the very act of dipping in the same dish with Him.

Still the heart of Judas remained untouched, and he

continued his wicked course, even when the mournful accents of the tender Voice fell on his ear, "Betrayest thou the Son of Man with a kiss?." Who can wonder at the fearful ending to the story? We can only thank God that Judas repented, and even bore testimony to the innocence of Him Whom he had betrayed.

But from thenceforth in the Anglican Church "the same night that He was betrayed" has been perpetually commemorated in union with the One Great Sacrifice of the Altar by the words of the Prayer of Consecration.

Thus are we called, even at that most solemn moment, to recall the suffering which our Blessed Lord endured in His betrayal, by the traitorous kiss of one who had been His companion and His friend.

May our meditations lead us to pray lest we, too, should betray Him Whom we love, and put Him to an open shame.

The greed of gain, the sin of covetousness, are not sins of a bygone age. They tempt us now as they tempted Judas then, and the Holy Spirit alone can keep us in the Love and Truth of Christ.

> "Be Thou my Guardian and my Guide,
>   And hear me when I call;
> Let not my slippery footsteps slide,
>   And hold me lest I fall.
>
> And if I tempted am to sin,
>   And outward things are strong,
> Do Thou, O Lord, keep watch within,
>   And save my soul from wrong."

Aspiration.
"*Lead us not into temptation.*"

Voice of Jesus.
LET HIM THAT THINKETH HE STANDETH TAKE HEED LEST HE FALL."

Read *Psalm xli.* Lesson, *S. Luke xxii.* 47-54.

Litany of the Passion.

Wednesday before Easter.

DESPISED.

"ALL THEY THAT SEE ME LAUGH ME TO SCORN."—PSALM XXII. 7.

"LOVE YOUR ENEMIES, BLESS THEM THAT CURSE YOU, DO GOOD TO THEM THAT HATE YOU, AND PRAY FOR THEM WHICH DESPITEFULLY USE YOU AND PERSECUTE YOU."—S. MATT. V. 44.

"*Son, cast thy heart firmly on the Lord, and fear not the judgment of man, when thy conscience gives testimony of thy piety and innocence.*

"*It is good and happy to suffer in this manner, neither will this be grievous to an humble heart, nor to him that trusts in God more than in himself.*

"*Though Paul endeavoured to please all in the Lord, and made himself all unto all; yet he made little account of his being judged by the judgment of men.*

"*He laboured for the edification and salvation of others as much as he could, and as lay in him; but he could not prevent his being sometimes judged or despised by others.*

"*If at present thou seem to be overcome, and to suffer a confusion which thou hast not deserved, do not repine at this, and do not lessen thy crown by impatience.*

"*Be not dismayed with the labours which thou hast undertaken for Me; neither let the tribulations which befall thee quite cast thee down; but let My Promise strengthen thee, and comfort thee.*"   *THOMAS A KEMPIS.*

Let us to-day consider Him that "endured such contradiction of sinners against Himself, lest we be wearied and faint in our minds."

What is more wearying to the mind than scorn and contempt, especially if they are directed against that which is most sacred in our eyes, and most dear to our hearts?

Mockery, and ridicule, and sarcasm, are weapons of the Prince of evil, and they are cruel, and inflict grievous wounds, so that when we are exposed to them we cry out sometimes that our "whole head is sick, and our whole heart faint."

In such moments of depression and misery, let us consider the Man of Sorrows, and see how He bore to be despised and rejected of men. See Him exposed to the coarse insults of brutal heathen soldiers, see Him, the Lord of Glory, buffeted, blindfolded, spit upon; mocked and taunted with the possession He held most dear, His Sonship to the Eternal Father, and yet He bore it all in silence and in patience, though myriads of Angels were waiting unseen around Him, and ready at any moment to reveal to the mocking crowd, their adoring homage to the Son of God.

Had He but raised His eyes above the hideous tumult and uproar which surrounded Him, the Heavens would have opened, and the Voice of the Eternal Father would have shaken the Heavens and the earth, and the mocking crowd would have been as dead men while the sound as of thunder smote upon their ears, "This is My Beloved Son, hear ye Him."

But then there would have been no cross of suffering, and no crown of reward for those who follow the Lamb.

So for our sakes the dear Master kept silence before His accusers, and "hid not His Face from shame and spitting."

Therefore let us adore Him, and let us for His sake be ready to be despised of all men, and gladly to follow Him out of the city, bearing His reproach.

> "Oft in life's stillest shade reclining,
> In desolation unrepining,
> Without a hope on earth to find
> A mirror in an answering mind.
> Meek souls there are who little dream
> Their daily strife an angel's theme,
> Or that the rod they take so calm
> Shall prove in Heaven a martyr's palm."

> "'O Father, not My Will, but Thine be done,'
> So spoke the Son;
> Be this our charm, mellowing earth's ruder noise
> Of griefs and joys,
> That we may cling for ever to Thy Breast
> In perfect rest."

Aspiration.
"Lord, shall we smite with the sword?"

Voice of Jesus.
"THE CUP THAT MY FATHER HATH GIVEN ME, SHALL I NOT DRINK IT?"

Read *Psalm xciv.* Lesson, *Isa. liii.*

Litany of the Passion.

Thursday before Easter.

CARRYING HIS CROSS.

"THE POOR SHALL EAT AND BE SATISFIED! THEY THAT SEEK AFTER THE LORD SHALL PRAISE HIM."—PSALM XXII. 26.

"AS OFTEN AS YE EAT THIS BREAD AND DRINK THIS CUP YE DO SHOW THE LORD'S DEATH TILL HE COME."—I COR. XI. 26.

" *If thou carry the cross willingly, it will carry thee and bring thee to thy desired end: to wit, to that place where there will be an end to suffering, though here there will be no end.*

" *If thou carry it unwillingly, thou makest it a burden to thee, and loadest thyself the more; and nevertheless thou must bear it.*

" *If thou fling away one cross, no doubt thou shalt find another, and perhaps a heavier.*

" *Our Lord Jesus Christ Himself was not one hour of His life without suffering: thus it behoved Christ to suffer, saith He.*

" *And how dost thou pretend to seek another way than this Royal way, which is the Way of the Holy Cross?*

" *Thou commandest me to approach to Thee with confidence, if I would have part with Thee; and to receive the Food of Immortality, if I desire to obtain life and glory everlasting.*"   THOMAS A KEMPIS.

THIS Holy Thursday, so near to the Cross as it stands, shines in the story of the Passion with a threefold glory, for on this day it behoves us to meditate on three of the glorious incidents of the last days of our dear Lord's Life on earth—the new commandment which He gave His disciples, after He had washed their feet, from which the name "Maundy Thursday" comes;—the institution of the ever-blessed Sacrament of His Body and His Blood—and the journey of the Lord out of Jerusalem to Golgotha bearing His Cross. Many other most sad and beautiful subjects of thought are there for every hour of these sacred days, and each one of us can meditate on that which touches our own heart most nearly.

Let us to-day fall down before Him and adore Him in that Great Sacrament, by means of Which He has continued in all ages to be still Present among us, and wherein we do show forth His Death continually until His coming again.

In that Most Holy Feast, too, may we learn the great lesson of the Charity of God, for it is in a very special manner the Feast of Love; in It the two chords of love are mixed in one sweet harmony of praise, love to God and love to our brethren for the Lord's sake—love which is ever ascending from us to Heaven, like the angels in Jacob's Vision, and like them descends upon us again in the Benediction of the Love of God. To-day may the new commandment be ever ringing in our ears, "Little children, love one another."

With hearts full of love to God and to our neighbour, with our bodies and souls washed from all pollution and all sin, and fed and strengthened with the Precious Food of Angels let us follow our dear Master out of the city, rejoicing indeed if we be counted worthy to bear with Him, the weight of the Cross.

> "O, taste and see, O, taste and see !
> How gracious Jesus is to thee ;
> As honey dropped upon the ground,
> So in His Sacrament is found
> Celestial sweetness stored for thee,
> O, taste my spirit, taste and see.

"O, Manna pure! O, precious Wine,
True Blood of Him Who is the Vine,
Memorials that can never cease,
The Corn and Wine that must increase.
Thy Saviour gives Himself to thee;
O, taste, my spirit, taste and see."

Aspiration.

"*Why can I not follow Thee now?*"

Voice of Jesus.

"WHITHER I GO THOU CANST NOT FOLLOW ME NOW, BUT THOU SHALT FOLLOW ME AFTERWARDS."

Read *Psalm lxxxi.* Lesson, *S. John vi. 30 to 41.*

Litany of the Passion.

Good Friday.

GLORIOUS IN HIS APPAREL.

"THEY PART MY GARMENTS AMONG THEM: AND CAST LOTS UPON MY VESTURE."—PSALM XXII. 18.

"WHO IS THIS THAT COMETH FROM EDOM, WITH DYED GARMENTS FROM BOZRAH, THIS THAT IS GLORIOUS IN HIS APPAREL?"—ISA. LXIII. 1.

" *Let Heaven and earth, with all their attire, be silent in Thy Presence, O my dearest Beloved; for whatever praise or beauty they have, is all the gift of Thy Bounty; nor can they come up to the Beauty of Thy Name of Whose wisdom there is no end.*

" *Behold, eating, drinking, clothing and other necessaries appertaining to the support of the body, are burdensome to a fervent spirit.*

" O my God, let not flesh and blood prevail over me, let it not overcome me; let not the world and its transitory glory deceive me.

" Give me fortitude, that I may stand my ground; patience, that I may endure; and constancy, that I may persevere."
THOMAS A KEMPIS.

On this most solemn of all days in the Christian year, let us be very still, and silent, and quiet, in the Presence of the awful Mystery of the Crucifixion. Let us meditate for a little while on one incident which seems so small, and yet we shall do well to consider it, because it will help to prepare our hearts to spend the sacred "three hours" more close to our dying Lord.

" They put His own garments on Him and led Him out to crucify Him." He wore His own raiment at His crucifixion, just His everyday apparel, the clothes which He wore when He rode into Jerusalem, the garment probably which had been touched by the sufferer in the crowd, and had been the means of her cure, the same He had worn when He washed the Disciples' feet, and when He knelt in Gethsemane.

Whence, then, came the glorious apparel in which the prophetic vision saw Him arrayed?

His raiment was stained with His own most Precious Blood, hence all the beauty and the glory of its dye.

In Gethsemane,—at the pillar of scourging,—from the crown of thorns,—those life-giving drops fell and stained all His raiment. Glorious indeed was the apparel dyed with the Blood of Jesus, in which He went forth to die.

May it be given to us to die in the simplicity of our working garb, made sacred by toil for Christ, and sanctified by our suffering with Him, and when this life is ended, may

He welcome us to His Presence, and give us garments clean and pure, white robes that have been washed in the Blood of the Lamb.

> "Sweet the moments, rich in blessing,
> Which before the Cross I spend?
> Life, and health, and peace possessing
> From the sinner's dying Friend.
>
> Here I rest for ever viewing
> Mercy's stream in streams of blood;
> Precious drops my soul bedewing,
> Plead and claim my peace with God.
>
> Love and grief my heart dividing,
> With my tears His feet I'll bathe;
> Constant still in faith abiding,
> Life deriving from His death."

Aspiration.

"*Thou wast slain, and hast redeemed us to God by Thy Blood.*"

Voice of Jesus.

"HE THAT OVERCOMETH, THE SAME SHALL BE CLOTHED IN WHITE RAIMENT."

Read *Psalm xlv.* Lesson, *Rev. xix. 1 to 9.*

Litany of the Passion.

Easter Eve.

RESTING FROM HIS LABOURS.

"SO HE GIVETH HIS BELOVED SLEEP."—PSALM CXXVII. 2.
"WE WHICH HAVE BELIEVED DO ENTER INTO REST."—HEB. IV. 3.

> "*Above all things, and in all things, do thou, my soul, rest always in the Lord, for He is the Eternal Rest of the Saints.*
>
> "*Give me, O most sweet and loving Jesus, to repose in Thee above all things created, above all health and beauty, above all glory and honour, above all power and dignity, above all knowledge and subtlety, above all riches and arts, above all joy and gladness, above all fame and praise, above all sweetness and consolation, above all hope and promise, above all merit and desire, above all the gifts and presents that Thou canst give and impart, above all the joy and jubilation that the mind can contain and experience; in fine, above all angels and archangels, and all the hosts of Heaven; above all things visible and invisible, and above all that which is less than Thee, my God.*
>
> "*For Thou, O Lord my God, art the best above all things; Thou alone most high; Thou alone most sufficient and most full; Thou alone most sweet and most full of consolation.*
>
> "*My heart cannot truly rest, nor be entirely contented, till it rest in Thee, and rise above all things created.*
>
> "*O my most Beloved Spouse, Christ Jesus, Who will give me the wings of true liberty to fly and repose in Thee, when shall it be fully granted me to attend at leisure, and see how sweet Thou art, O Lord my God?*"
>
> THOMAS A KEMPIS.

To-day may our souls rest with Jesus, and wait patiently on Him, ready with a pure heart, and a love unfeigned, to welcome Him to-morrow, when He comes at the early dawn, to give Himself to us.

During our Lenten Meditations we have seen that religion is not a system of running about from one so-called "good work" to another, but it is the study of the nature, the works and ways of God, and the ruling of our lives thereby. Without study and meditation and thinking upon God, it is impossible to please Him, for while in our unprepared state of hurry and anxiety we rush off to set things right which we believe to be wrong, the home of our heart is left unprotected, and the enemy comes in and takes possession of it.

The soul that waits upon God must have long patience for Him—it must live its life in silence and in quiet, alone with God, buried from the world, dead to self, out of sight of men, but abiding in the Presence of the Lord.

In this way those who believe may, even in this noisy and turbulent world, " enter into their rest."

" In the sight of the world they seem to die, and their departure is counted as misery, but they are at rest."

Peace is the last, best, gift which was purchased for us by the Blood of Jesus.

It is the precious benediction of the Seventh day, it is the consummation and the crown of the six days' toil. It does not belong to earth, it is only Jesus Who can bring it there. Angels' songs proclaimed it at His Birth, He bequeathed it to His children at His death, and He gives it to them daily in His great and holy Feast of Love and Peace.

Let us to-day muse in silence by the grave of Jesus, and gather beside His garden sepulchre, sweet flowers of peace and calm to soothe us in this troublesome world, and to make joyful the hour of our death.

> " Like that wondrous hush o'er Eden,
> When all the six days' toil was done,
> And God His mighty work approving,
> The first of Sabbaths had begun.
>
> So all His pains and sorrows ended,
> His work of man's redemption done;
> Now resting from His new creation
> Sleeps in the tomb th' Eternal Son.

"Soft laid in earth's dark silent bosom,
'Neath flowers that kissed His living Feet,
He sleeps, while angels watch in silence
His waking with their songs to greet."

Aspiration.
"*Come, Lord Jesus.*"

Voice of Jesus.
"PEACE I LEAVE WITH YOU, MY PEACE I GIVE UNTO YOU."

Read *Psalm xlix.*   Lesson, *Rev. xiv. 12 to 17.*

Litany of the Passion.

LAUS DEO.

APPENDIX.

Litany of Patience.

Lord have pity on us.
Jesus have pity on us.
Lord have pity on us.
Jesus hear us.
Jesus help us.

Heavenly Father, Who art patient because Thou art Eternal,
    Give me patience.
My Saviour and my God, Who sought me when I fled from Thee,
Spirit of Grace, Who has been with me to this day,
Holy Trinity, my Support in all my miseries,
    Give me patience.
Lord, when Thou tryest me,
Lord, when I am in need,
Lord, when I suffer from cold or heat,
    Give me patience.
Lord, when I suffer from illness,
Lord, when my members are racked with pain,
Lord, when I sufler, and cannot sleep,
    Give me patience.
Lord, in all my afflictions,
Lord, when the enemy comes against me,
Lord, when my spirit is desolate,
    Give me patience.

Appendix.

Lord, when I am on the point of falling,
When I cannot subdue my spirit,
When through tribulation I am weary of my life,
> Give me patience.

When I feel myself a burden to myself and others,
When all seems dark around me,
When in spite of my efforts I fall again and again into the same faults,
> Give me patience, Lord.

When my soul is overcome by fear,
When all fervour is dried up,
When distractions assail me at time of prayer,
> Give me patience, Lord.

When sin contends against grace within me,
If Thou permittest me to be contradicted and thwarted,
If Thou permittest me to be misunderstood and wrongly judged,
If Thou permittest others to be set against me,
> Give me patience, Lord.

If Thou permittest me to be humiliated by my superiors,
If Thou permittest that I am rebelled against by inferiors,
If Thou permittest that I am forsaken by my friends,
> Give me patience, Lord.

If Thou permittest that I be abused by my enemies,
If Thou permittest me to suffer injustice,
If Thou permittest that I be ridiculed and mocked,
> Give me patience, Lord.

If Thou permittest that I receive evil for good,
If Thou permittest that evil men should lie in wait for me,
If Thou permittest me to suffer injury and insult,
> Give me patience, Lord.

Lamb of God, Who takest away the sins of the world;
> Spare us, Lord, and give us patience evermore.
>> Amen.

www.ingramcontent.com/pod-product-compliance
Lightning Source LLC
Chambersburg PA
CBHW031348160426
43196CB00007B/772